Bots, Bias, and Influence

Bots, Bias, and Influence:

The Hidden Architects of Social Media

By

Lynnette Hui Xian Ng
and Kathleen M. Carley

Cambridge Scholars
Publishing

Bots, Bias, and Influence: The Hidden Architects of Social Media

By Lynnette Hui Xian Ng and Kathleen M. Carley

This book first published 2026

Cambridge Scholars Publishing

Lady Stephenson Library, Newcastle upon Tyne, NE6 2PA, UK

British Library Cataloguing in Publication Data
A catalogue record for this book is available from the British Library

ISBN: 978-1-0364-7310-5
ISBN (Ebook): 978-1-0364-7311-2

DEDICATION AND ACKNOWLEDGMENTS

To everyone for believing in me first, and not letting me give up.
-- Lynnette Hui Xian Ng

This book emerged out of almost two decades of work exploring information diffusion and influence in social media in the center for Computational Analysis of Social and Organizational Systems (CASOS) and the center for Informed Democracy and Social-cyber Security at Carnegie Mellon University. Every PhD student in those centers did some research that informed the perspective and understanding of information diffusion, belief change, human-machine teaming in the online and offline world. We especially want to acknowledge these students, friends and colleagues for their suggestions, for listening to numerous presentations about bots, and for doing some of the fundamental research that made this book possible. In particular, we want to acknowledge the many contributions of David Beskow who wrote the first handbook to bots, and wrote the original bot-hunter. This work fundamentally builds on his initial foray into the Bot world.

This material is based upon work supported by the Scalable Technologies for Social Cybersecurity, U.S. Army (W911NF20D0002), the Threat Assessment Techniques for Digital Data, Office of Naval Research (N000142412414), and the MURI: Persuasion, Identity & Morality in Social-Cyber Environments (N000142112749), Office of Naval Research. The views and conclusions contained in this book are those of the authors and should not be interpreted as representing official policies, either expressed or implied by the Office of Naval Research, U.S. Army or the U.S. government.

Digital conversations on social media are more than just human voices. Automated agents called Bots now weave themselves into our conversations and our collective beliefs. This book takes readers on an exploration of how Bots span simple automated scripts to complex agents that mirror, magnify and manipulate human behaviour online. Drawing on rich empirical data, social psychology theories and computational modelling, it traces how Bots operate, coordinate and exert influence through narrative construction, network embedding and psychological exploitation. From harmless announcer Bots to sophisticated networked Bots operating across global geographies, this book unpacks the taxonomy of digital agents that cohabit our online spaces. It offers an interdisciplinary approach for understanding the technical capabilities of Bots and their social consequences. It speaks to scholars and curious readers alike, arguing that Bots are not merely malicious actors but sociotechnical agents capable of both harm and good, whose impact depends on how we design, govern and coexist with them.

TABLE OF CONTENTS

PREFACE

The boundaries of cyberspace are not solely occupied by humans. Today, a parallel society thrives within our social media platforms: Bots. Social Media Bot, software-driven entities programmed by humans that operate autonomously, are more than mere tools. They have become a species of their own, with unique traits and an expanding array of personas. This book begins its journey with PepitoTheCat, a simple yet beloved Bot created in 2011 to chronicle the comings and goings of its feline namesake. With each automated update, Pepito's world has grown from a home automation experiment into a dynamic node of creativity and connection, giving rise to a whole micro-ecosystem of Bots with diverse logics and personas, from announcers to conversational companions. As social media platforms evolved to support not just text but also video and audio, so too did bots.

The presence and impact of Bots are far-reaching. No longer passive devices, Bots shape online communities, initiate conversations, participate in artistic challenges, and even serve as datasets for cutting-edge AI research. As Bots interact with each other and with humans, they mirror and amplify the behaviors, biases, and emotions inherent in digital discourse. The statistics are staggering: on major platforms like X and Facebook, Bots account for millions, sometimes billions, of users, actively influencing the presentation, perception, and spread of information. Their proliferation is accelerating, making them ever more central to the collective digital experience. Their ability to mimic human behavior is improving, making them more influential, harder to detect, and more of a team member in the human-machine ecosystem.

Behind the curtain of automated posts lies the strategic use of Bots as agents of influence—for better or worse. From benevolent information disseminators to orchestrators of large-scale propaganda campaigns, Bots can amplify useful facts during crises or manipulate the collective psyche through disinformation, emotional triggers, and bias reinforcement. The entanglement of automation and human cognition creates powerful feedback loops, making it increasingly urgent to understand not just what Bots are, but why they matter. It is important to understand how bots can be used for good, how humans can partner with, and how they can be used for nefarious purposes.

This book is a guide through the complex world of social media Bots. It explores the interplay of technical innovation and psychological vulnerability, maps the behavioral patterns and operational mechanics of digital agents, and surveys their multifaceted role in shaping public discourse. By weaving together synthetic scenarios, like AuraSight's contested song contest, and real-life case studies, the chapters provide grounded insight into the bot-human dynamics at play in modern online networks.

"Bots, Bias and Influence" is a resource for social media enthusiasts, researchers, and practitioners alike. It aims to equip readers with a comprehensive understanding of automated accounts, their mechanics, and their impact across platforms. In charting the invisible architectures that Bots construct, this book invites new perspectives and ideas for maintaining a healthier, more resilient online ecosystem.

LIST OF ILLUSTRATIONS

LIST OF TABLES

1

BOTS, BIAS AND INFLUENCE

Humans are not the only species that exist in cyberspace. Social Media Bots, or Bots for short, exist alongside us. The Bot species, while created by humans, operates automatically. Like humans, this species has its own characteristics, and a diverse set of personas.

This chapter lays out the key ideas and the scope of the study of Bot detection and influence, to familiarize the reader with the social media landscape that Bots live in.

Introduction

PepitoTheCat is a Bot account on the X platform created in 2011 that tracks the movements of Pepito, a black cat[1]. Pepito's owner, Clement Storck, constructed a device to monitor his cat's movement. Each entry or exit that Pepito makes through his cat door triggers the account to tweet "Pepito is out" or "Pepito is back home", along with a photo and the timestamp. *PepitoTheCat* is an example of an Announcer Bot archetype, where an event automatically triggers a social media post.

Over time, *PepitoTheCat* has grown beyond a simple home automation project into a beloved online animal presence that inspires community interaction and creative participation. The account has enabled the #PepitoArtChallenge hashtag to trend, where users share fan art of the cat, and imagine stories about his adventures. Other users harvest the image data captured as datasets for computer vision tasks, for example, analyzing Pepito's emotions from the images.

PepitoTheCat does not live on his own. He has companion Bots that highlight different automation logics and personas. *pepitosfriend* is another

---

[1] https://www.newscientist.com/article/mg26735574-200-anyone-keen-on-a-cat-cryptocoin-anyone/

conversational Bot on X. She reacts to Pepito's movements by asking where Pepito is going for his adventure when he leaves his house. If she does not hear from Pepito for some time, she asks after Pepito's well-being[2]. *PepitoSecFriend*, by contrast, is a repeater and announcer Bot that follows a consistent schedule and uses a post template. He posts "Where is Pepito? I miss him!! (timestamp)" every two hours, regardless of Pepito's actual activity[3].

This micro-ecosystem of cat-related Bots of Pepito and friends illustrate the diversity of social media Bot archetypes. Over the years, Bot accounts have evolved to become a species of its own, exhibiting a variety of distinct behavioral signatures and a spectrum of personalities and operational capabilities. Some Bots are like a broken record and endlessly repeat themselves; other bots are more like social butterflies, interacting with several social communities. Bots no longer function merely as tools (like the original *PepitoTheCat*), but as active participants in online ecosystems, initiating conversations, responding to unfolding events and forming relationships with other accounts, both human and automated.

Academic studies estimate that 8-18% of users on X are Bots[4]. In 2025, Meta's own reports indicated about 3% of the active users were inauthentic[5]. This accounted for almost a billion accounts. These figures are not static; in fact, they have grown over time. In May 2021, X's filing with the US Securities and Exchange Commission states that 3-5% of its daily active users are Bots[6]. By May 2025, independent analyses suggests that the proportion of Bots in X ranges from 12% to as high as 64%[7], reflecting both

---

[2] https://www.vice.com/en/article/why-this-cat-is-more-famous-than-you-pepito-twitter/

[3] https://x.com/pepitosecfriend

[4] Fukuda, Mei, Kazuki Nakajima, and Kazuyuki Shudo. "Estimating the bot population on Twitter via random walk based sampling." *IEEE Access* 10 (2022): 17201-17211.; Varol, Onur, Emilio Ferrara, Clayton Davis, Filippo Menczer, and Alessandro Flammini. "Online human-bot interactions: Detection, estimation, and characterization." In *Proceedings of the international AAAI conference on web and social media*, vol. 11, no. 1, pp. 280-289. 2017.

[5] Meta Transparency Center. Community Standards Enforcement Report Q1 2025, Fake Accounts.
https://transparency.meta.com/reports/community-standards-enforcement/fake-accounts/facebook/

[6] https://www.sec.gov/Archives/edgar/data/1418091/000141809122000029/twtr-20211231.htm

[7] https://x.com/grok/status/1927532839999824198

the rapid growth of the Bot species and the challenges of accurately measuring their numbers.

When deployed at large scale, Bots are capable of shaping discourse and influencing public perception, sometimes for bad, sometimes for good. Operation Rising Lion was a large-scale Bot driven campaign launched by Iran that was discovered in 2025[8]. This information campaign consisted of over 100 Bots on X that posted thousands of messages daily. The Bots presented a coordinated effort to promote loyalty to the Iranian regime, showcased fabricated reports of Israeli military failures, and promoted anti-Semitic messaging targeted towards Israeli-Americans and Jewish-Americans. This Bot network intended to enhance Iran's international image while eroding the credibility of opposing groups like Israel.

So, what is a **Social Media Bot**, or more ubiquitously known as a **Bot**? The term Bot is a shortened form of the word "Robot". Wikipedia defines a robot as "a machine – especially one programmable by a computer – capable of carrying out a complex series of actions automatically"[9]. Many of us are familiar with the physical embodiment of a robot, influenced by movies and television shows. BB-8 and C3PO are beloved robots from the Star Wars franchise that aid their masters in navigation, communication, daily tasks, and even survival. Similarly, in the digital realm, social media Bots are programmed to talk and interact on online platforms. Instead of helping humans to repair a spaceship, these Bots automate information flows or amplify messages, or carry out information operations, making them important actors in modern information ecosystems.

Put simply, a Bot is a social media account run by software rather than a human. **Definition 1.1** states the formal definition of a Bot, that was formulated by harmonizing definitions from academic papers and industry terminologies. The software automates and controls the processing and delivering of social media content, operating on pre-programmed coded instructions rather than spontaneous human thought.

Definition 1.1: A **Social Media Bot** is an automated account that carries out a series of mechanics on social media platforms, for content creation,

---

[8] https://nypost.com/2025/07/02/world-news/iranian-bots-posted-240k-times-to-block-us-strikes

[9] https://en.wikipedia.org/wiki/Robot

distribution and collection, and/or for relationship formation and dissolutions[10].

Understanding *what* a Bot is, and *how many* Bots are only the first step. The more pressing question is *why* these Bots matter, and why this species demands sustained study. Bots are not peripheral actors of human creation; they are woven into the fabric of online discourse, capable of shaping conversations and perceptions. Their influence can be either positive, as in dissemination of useful information during crisis[11], or negative, when they persuade humans to believe misinformation[12]. Human cognitive biases play a role in this influence dynamic. These biases are mental shortcuts that humans take to cope with the processing of overwhelming digital information[13]. For example, confirmation bias on is the inclination to believe information that matches one's prior beliefs, a bias that creates echo-chambers as people continually interact with content they are familiar with[14]. These shortcuts in mental processing make individuals more susceptible to persuasive tactics.

Bots can deliberately embed cognitive triggers into their content to influence how people engage with their posts, architecting the overall perception of information. For example, negativity bias is the inclination for people to more easily believe negative news, and Bots activate this bias by repeating inflammatory and negative narratives, spiking exposure of the

---

[10] Ng, Lynnette Hui Xian, and Kathleen M. Carley. "A global comparison of social media bot and human characteristics." *Scientific Reports* 15, no. 1 (2025): 10973.

[11] Hofeditz, Lennart, Christian Ehnis, Deborah Bunker, Florian Brachten, and Stefan Stieglitz. "Meaningful use of social bots? Possible applications in crisis communication during disasters." (2019).

[12] Ross, Björn, Laura Pilz, Benjamin Cabrera, Florian Brachten, German Neubaum, and Stefan Stieglitz. "Are social bots a real threat? An agent-based model of the spiral of silence to analyse the impact of manipulative actors in social networks." *European Journal of Information Systems* 28, no. 4 (2019): 394-412.

[13] Tversky, Amos, and Daniel Kahneman. "Judgment under Uncertainty: Heuristics and Biases: Biases in judgments reveal some heuristics of thinking under uncertainty." *science* 185, no. 4157 (1974): 1124-1131.

[14] Cinelli, Matteo, Gianmarco De Francisci Morales, Alessandro Galeazzi, Walter Quattrociocchi, and Michele Starnini. "The echo chamber effect on social media." *Proceedings of the national academy of sciences* 118, no. 9 (2021): e2023301118.

narratives and increasing belief and memory of the narrative[15]. The interplay between automation, bias and emotions creates powerful feedback loops for influence dynamics: Bots target susceptible audiences, and audiences engage in ways to reinforce the Bots' narratives, resulting in activity that signal credibility and popularity of user and narrative to the wider social network. This cycle is central to how Bots exert influence, making it vital to study both their technical characteristics and psychological vulnerabilities they exploit. Note that in this book, a **social network** is defined as the network that represents the social communication between users through nodes and links in a graph, rather than the platforms "Facebook", "Instagram", "X" and so forth.

This book examines both the social and computational aspects of social media Bots. We approach the study of Bots through the lens of social personalities and social media interactions. We characterize the content-based and behavioral-based persona types of Bots, analyze the formation of Bot-Bot and Bot-human communication networks. We also connect the technological mechanics of automation with the psychological underpinnings of human decision making, exploring how Bots leverage cognitive biases to shape perceptions and drive engagement. The entanglement of Bots with the online human society enable them to use their capabilities to influence digital conversations in constructive ways, by promoting beneficial information and fostering community, or detrimental ways, by amplifying misinformation or polarizing discourse. This book, *Bots, Bias and Influence: The Hidden Architects of Social Media*, maps the intersection of technology, human psychology and communication theory, providing a comprehensive framework for understanding the role of Bots in the modern information ecosystem.

Scenario and Data Used in This Book

To explore these Bot-human dynamics in a controlled, observable setting, most of the concepts in this book are illustrated with a synthetic social media network, AuraSight[16]. AuraSight is generated through a hybrid modeling framework that combines Agent-Based Modeling (ABM) and Large-

---

[15] Stella, Massimo, Emilio Ferrara, and Manlio De Domenico. "Bots increase exposure to negative and inflammatory content in online social systems." *Proceedings of the National Academy of Sciences* 115, no. 49 (2018): 12435-12440.

[16] Ng, Lynnette Hui Xian, Bianca NY Kang, and Kathleen M. Carley. "AuraSight: Generating Realistic Social Media Data." *Center for the Computational Analysis of Social and Organizational Systems* (2025).

Language-Model (LLM) generation. This fictional scenario simulates the interactions of human users and various classes of Bot accounts in a realistic social network structure that mirrors the clustering, community formation and information diffusion dynamics observed in real-world social media data. The central conflict in AuraSight centers on Oliver, the unexpected winner of a national song contest, sparking rivalry among fans, nationalists and bots working to amplify or discredit competing narratives. There are two countries: Odria, the country which Oliver represents, and Ethal, a country that fielded two representatives, Ezekiel and Ella, who lost to Oliver. There are therefore two sides to this story, both promoting their own faction and booing the other faction.

Sometimes, we also use real-life examples to enhance our points. For such examples, we use descriptions of activity of public accounts, and do not reproduce any social media posts. This is to respect user privacy settings. Public accounts are accounts that are not restricted or protected.

Organization of this Book

Bots, Bias and Influence: The Hidden Architects of Social Media aims to bring together researchers, practitioners and social media platform providers in the understanding of the online ecosystem by providing an in-depth characterization and analysis of the automated Bot accounts that exist in the social media space, particularly exploring how they leverage human cognitive biases and wield influence as the hidden architects in shaping conversations and narratives across social media platforms.

This book aims to be a general reading material for those interested in social media, in particular, automated Bot accounts. It hopes to provide a broad overview for understanding the mechanics and workings of the online landscape, and to provide background on the study of activity on social media platforms. Further, this book hopes to speak to researchers studying the interactions and behaviors of user types in online systems. We hope that researchers can build on our work and develop further techniques and ideas to maintain a healthy online system.

2

BOT DETECTION

The first step of studying Bots is to identify them. Many Bot detection algorithms are concerned with providing a determination as to whether a given social media agent is a bot or a human. There are two main approaches of Bot detection algorithms: Bot detection by classification and Bot detection by clustering. Classification approaches treat Bot detection as a supervised learning task, first performing data engineering and feature extraction, then passing the feature vectors into a pre-trained machine learning model to output the probability that an account is a Bot or human. Clustering approaches adopt an unsupervised method by grouping accounts based on behavioral similarities such as the posting frequencies. Accounts that fall into unusually dense clusters are flagged as likely Bots. **Figure 2.1** provides an illustration to the concept of Bot detection by classification and clustering.

This chapter first provides an overview of some of the existing Bot detection techniques in the literature, and the more commercially available tools. It then elaborates on how Bots rarely act in isolation, but instead operate as Bot networks, using coordination techniques to amplify their influence. Finally, the chapter concludes with a discussion on the responsible use of Bot detectors, emphasizing the risks of false positives, implications of labeling users and the importance of transparency in automated classification.

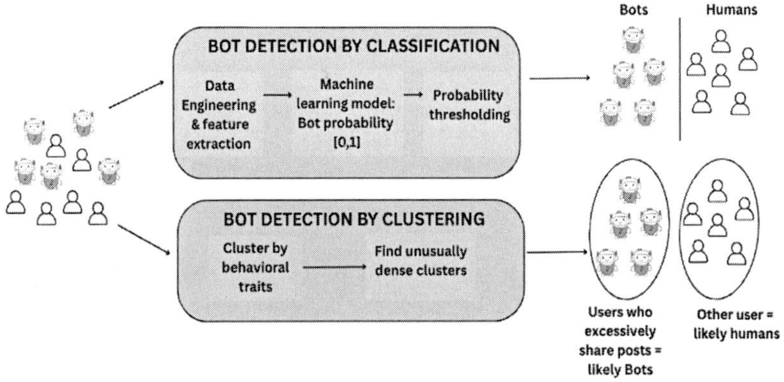

Figure 2.1: Illustration of the two approaches of Bot Detection algorithms

Bot Detection by Classification

Classification is the process of sorting objects into categories, or classes. For Bot detection, this means sorting users based on how likely they are to be Bots. To do this, Bot classification algorithms identify features that are typical of Bot behavior, such as posting patterns, content style, meta-data, or network structure. The algorithms then compare each user's features to these known Bot characteristics. The more closely a user's behavior matches these patterns, the more likely they are to be classified as a Bot.

Data engineering and feature extraction. The first part of a Bot detection by classification pipeline is data engineering and feature extraction. This involves manipulating the social media data to extract features that best represents an account, and optimizing the algorithm for the feature sets that best divides the data into the Bot/human class dichotomy. A significant amount of effort for designing a Bot detection classification algorithm is spent in the first stage of feature engineering. These feature set range from user meta-data features (i.e., location, presence of profile pictures, posting patterns) to content-based features (i.e. linguistic structure, syntactic structure) to interaction features (i.e., how many other Bot accounts they follow). A canonical example is the Botometer algorithm, which aggregates over 1000 features that includes content, sentiment, friend/follower the user, tweet and relationships for the Bot classification task[25]. Graph-Hist explores latent feature histograms for graph classification which demonstrated strong performance (95%) accuracy in the Bot detection task[26].

Most recently, Large Language Models (LLMs) have been explored as tools for Bot classification. Unlike earlier approaches that rely heavily on feature engineering, LLMs leverage a large pool of contextual knowledge that they are being trained with, and distinguish Bot-generated with human-authored texts using their understanding of language. For example, LMBot distills knowledge from GNNs into a pre-trained language model[27]. At inference time, the Bot detection is performed without the need to transverse a graph data but still using information gathered from the constructed graph. This method produced an accuracy of 98-99%. Instruction-tuned LLMs have been able to classify Bots with high accuracy (76-89%)[28]. These LLMs are also accurate even when fine-tuned on as few as 1,000 annotated examples, which reduces the manual labor required to collect and label Bots.

Many of these algorithms differ in terms of (1) the source of their data, i.e., whether they use historical or require live data; and (2) amount of data required. The different use of data source and amount of data required for some algorithms are listed in **Table 2.1.**

---

[25] Feng, Shangbin, Herun Wan, Ningnan Wang, Jundong Li, and Minnan Luo. "Twibot-20: A comprehensive twitter bot detection benchmark." In *Proceedings of the 30th ACM international conference on information & knowledge management*, pp. 4485-4494. 2021. ; Feng, Shangbin, Zhaoxuan Tan, Herun Wan, Ningnan Wang, Zilong Chen, Binchi Zhang, Qinghua Zheng et al. "Twibot-22: Towards graph-based twitter bot detection." *Advances in Neural Information Processing Systems* 35 (2022): 35254-35269.

[26] Magelinski, Thomas, David Beskow, and Kathleen M. Carley. "Graph-hist: Graph classification from latent feature histograms with application to bot detection." In *Proceedings of the AAAI Conference on Artificial Intelligence*, vol. 34, no. 04, pp. 5134-5141. 2020.

[27] Cai, Zijian, Zhaoxuan Tan, Zhenyu Lei, Zifeng Zhu, Hongrui Wang, Qinghua Zheng, and Minnan Luo. "LMbot: distilling graph knowledge into language model for graph-less deployment in twitter bot detection." In *Proceedings of the 17th ACM international conference on web search and data mining*, pp. 57-66. 2024.

[28] Feng, Shangbin, Herun Wan, Ningnan Wang, Zhaoxuan Tan, Minnan Luo, and Yulia Tsvetkov. "What Does the Bot Say? Opportunities and Risks of Large Language Models in Social Media Bot Detection." In *Proceedings of the 62nd Annual Meeting of the Association for Computational Linguistics (Volume 1: Long Papers)*, pp. 3580-3601. 2024.

The use of historical data means that the algorithm can use pre-existing data collection efforts, although the result of the algorithm may be dated. The algorithm makes a prediction of whether a user is a Bot or not based off the last collected data, and thus does not factor in account changes or if the account had been recently hijacked. The use of live data provides the most updated prediction of a user type, but most often requires data collection efforts and money.

The Bot detection algorithm also relies on data, and the type of data used can be conceptualized as a layered process like in **Figure 2.2**, where as one moves down the layers, more data is required. At the narrow top of the pyramid lie post-level features, such as the text of a single message, which requires relatively little data. Moving down, incorporating account metadata (i.e., user name, bio fields) add richer signals but requires collecting more information from the platform. Further layers like the timelines of posts, interaction patterns with friends, and finally the posts of those interactions expand the feature set, but also require larger volumes of data. With larger volumes of data comes increasing API, hardware costs and time to collect the data. However, features at the narrow top of the pyramid have little discriminative power, but when adding more features, the Bot detection algorithm becomes more reliable and comprehensive. Bot detection is thus a trade off between feature granularity and scope of data required, balancing efficiency against accuracy.

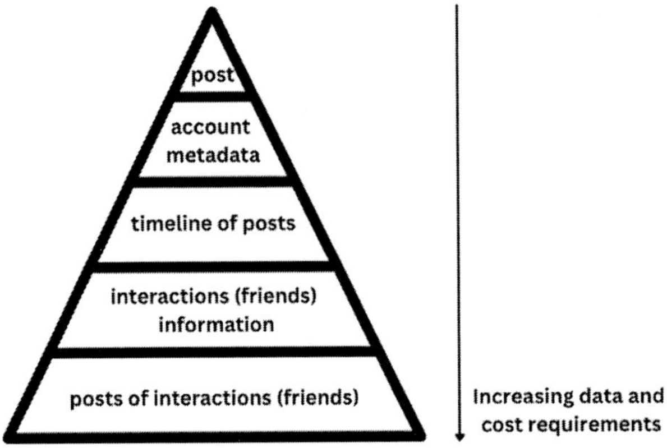

Figure 2.2: Increasing amounts of data and costs required for a Bot detection algorithm as more features are used.

Bot detection algorithm	Data Source	Amount of data required
BotHunter[29 30]	Historical	post, account metadata, timeline of posts, interactions (friends) information, posts of interactions (friends)
BotBuster[31]	Historical	post, account metadata
TwiBot-20, TwiBot-22[32]	Historical	post, account metadata, timeline of posts, interactions (friends) information, posts of interactions (friends)
Botometer[33]	Live data	post, account metadata, timeline of posts
Graph-Hist[34]	Historical	post, account metadata, timeline of posts, interactions (friends) information

Table 2.1: Summary of some Bot detection algorithms, their data source and the amount of data required

[29]Ng, Lynnette Hui Xian, Dawn C. Robertson, and Kathleen M. Carley. "Stabilizing a supervised bot detection algorithm: How much data is needed for consistent predictions?." *Online Social Networks and Media* 28 (2022): 100198.

[30] Beskow, David M., and Kathleen M. Carley. "Bot-hunter: a tiered approach to detection & characterizing automated activity on twitter." In conference paper. SBP-BRiMS: Interactional conference on social computing, behavioral-cultural modeling and prediction and behavior representation in modeling and simulation, vol. 3, no. 3. 2018

[31] Ng, Lynnette Hui Xian, and Kathleen M. Carley. "Botbuster: Multi-platform bot detection using a mixture of experts." In *Proceedings of the international AAAI conference on web and social media*, vol. 17, pp. 686-697. 2023.

[32] Feng, Shangbin, Herun Wan, Ningnan Wang, Jundong Li, and Minnan Luo. "Twibot-20: A comprehensive twitter bot detection benchmark." In *Proceedings of the 30th ACM international conference on information & knowledge management*, pp. 4485-4494. 2021. ; Feng, Shangbin, Zhaoxuan Tan, Herun Wan, Ningnan Wang, Zilong Chen, Binchi Zhang, Qinghua Zheng et al. "Twibot-22: Towards graph-based twitter bot detection." *Advances in Neural Information Processing Systems* 35 (2022): 35254-35269.

[33] Yang, Kai-Cheng, Emilio Ferrara, and Filippo Menczer. "Botometer 101: Social bot practicum for computational social scientists." Journal of computational social science 5, no. 2 (2022): 1511-1528.

[34] Magelinski, Thomas, David Beskow, and Kathleen M. Carley. "Graph-hist: Graph classification from latent feature histograms with application to bot detection." In *Proceedings of the AAAI Conference on Artificial Intelligence*, vol. 34, no. 04, pp. 5134-5141. 2020.

Probability thresholding. The final step of a Bot classification algorithm is probability thresholding. Bot classification algorithms typically return a probability score P(bot) between 0 and 1, to which a threshold ε is typically applied. If P(bot) is greater or equal to ε, the account is determined to be a Bot; if P(bot) is less than ε, then the account is determined to be a human. The problem with using such a threshold is that the threshold value affects the number and types of users that are being classified as a Bot. Too tight a threshold (i.e., a higher ε used) means that lesser users are classified as a Bot, and there will be more false negatives. Too loose a threshold (i.e., a lower ε used) means that more users will be classified as a Bot, and there will be more false positives.

Unfortunately, many studies use an arbitrary threshold value, which can result in instability and misclassification of users. In fact, even for the same algorithm, different threshold values are used for different studies. For the BotHunter algorithm, a study on hate speech and racism used the threshold value of 0.7 to differentiate Bots and humans[35], whereas a study on polarizing climate change narratives used a threshold value of 0.5[36].

One way to determine such a threshold value ε for a Bot classification algorithm is through a longitudinal analysis[37]. This approach applies the detection algorithm repeatedly to each user with an increasing number of posts. An effective threshold is one that minimizes false positives and yields consistency in classification. Classification consistency means that if the user is meant to be a Bot, it should be persistently classified as a Bot, and humans should be persistently classified as humans, rather than oscillating across labels with additional data. Using such longitudinal analysis, suitable

---

[35] Uyheng, Joshua, Daniele Bellutta, and Kathleen M. Carley. "Bots amplify and redirect hate speech in online discourse about racism during the COVID-19 pandemic." *Social Media+ Society* 8, no. 3 (2022): 20563051221104749.

[36] Tyagi, Aman, Matthew Babcock, Kathleen M. Carley, and Douglas C. Sicker. "Polarizing tweets on climate change." In *International Conference on Social Computing, Behavioral-Cultural Modeling and Prediction and Behavior Representation in Modeling and Simulation*, pp. 107-117. Cham: Springer International Publishing, 2020.

[37] Ng, Lynnette Hui Xian, Dawn C. Robertson, and Kathleen M. Carley. "Stabilizing a supervised bot detection algorithm: How much data is needed for consistent predictions?." *Online Social Networks and Media* 28 (2022): 100198.

thresholds for the BotHunter algorithm is ε=0.7, and a suitable threshold for the BotBuster algorithm is ε=0.5[38].

Bot Detection by Clustering

Clustering is the process of grouping objects together based on similarities. After the clustering process, objects that are in the same group are more similar to each other than they are to the objects in other groups. Bot detection by clustering aims to group users based on properties of social media mechanics. For example, if we group users based on the frequency of post creation, the social media mechanic is "post creation", and the property is "frequency".

To achieve this, clustering algorithms measure similarity across user behaviors then group accounts into sets that exhibit comparable patterns. The input features into such clustering algorithms include posting frequency, timing of activity, or interaction types. Each user is then represented as a multi-dimensional vector that indicates the occurrence of this feature. The algorithm then calculates distances or similarities between users in this feature space, then identifies dense clusters where many accounts behave in similar ways. These dense clusters are groups of users that are more alike to each other than to the users outside the cluster.

Figure 2.2 illustrates the network diagram of a single day of an all-communication network graph in the AuraSight scenario, the scenario generated for this book. In this network, nodes represent users, and links between two nodes represent that the two users communicated with each other. This communication can be re-tweeting each other or tagging each other in the post. The users were clustered by nationality, and the nodes were colored by nationality. This figure illustrates how clustering methods group together users of similar characteristics.

[38] Ng, Lynnette Hui Xian, Dawn C. Robertson, and Kathleen M. Carley. "Stabilizing a supervised bot detection algorithm: How much data is needed for consistent predictions?." *Online Social Networks and Media* 28 (2022): 100198. ; Ng, Lynnette Hui Xian, and Kathleen M. Carley. "Botbuster: Multi-platform bot detection using a mixture of experts." In *Proceedings of the international AAAI conference on web and social media*, vol. 17, pp. 686-697. 2023.

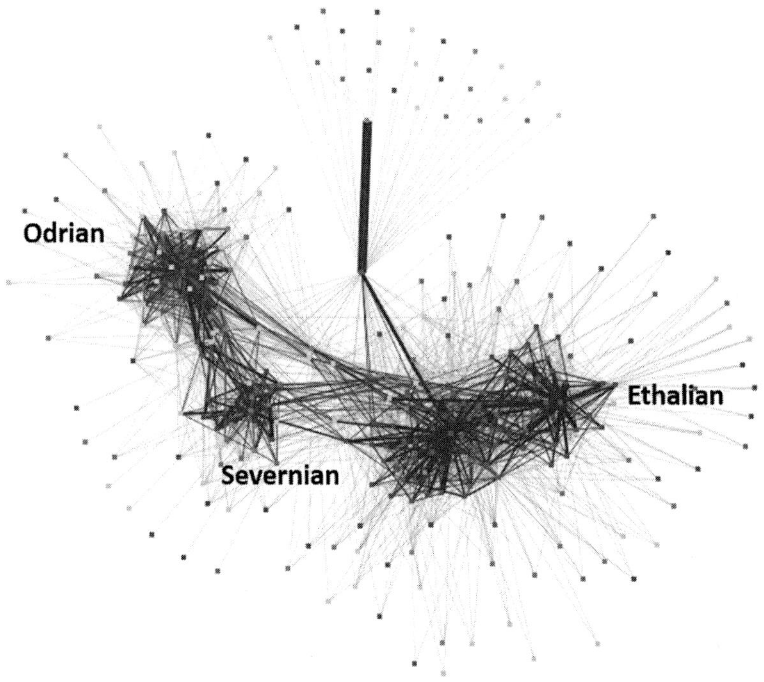

Figure 2.3: Illustration of network clusters of a day of an all-communication network graph in the AuraSight scenario. Nodes represent users, and links between two nodes represent that the two users communicated with each other (i.e., through retweet, user tags etc). These clusters of user interactions occur naturally by nationality.

Clustering by frequency of social media mechanics. One of the most straightforward ways to detect Bots through clustering is to group accounts by how frequently they engage in specific actions such as creating posts. Bots tend to post at a higher rate than human users, sometimes maintaining an almost continuous stream of activity, while humans generally show more irregular and limited posting patterns[39]. Such activity levels are typically unsustainable for human-operated accounts, because they require a fast and furious intensity, and an around-the-clock posting frequency that exceeds

---

[39] Pozzana, Iacopo, and Emilio Ferrara. "Measuring bot and human behavioral dynamics." *Frontiers in Physics* 8 (2020): 125. ; Chavoshi, Nikan, Hossein Hamooni, and Abdullah Mueen. "Temporal patterns in bot activities." In *Proceedings of the 26th international conference on world wide web companion*, pp. 1601-1606. 2017.

normal human behavior[40]. Bots use such heightened and continuous activity to exert influence in the social media sphere.

Empirically, studies found that the posting frequencies of Bots form distinct distributions from human patterns, which therefore allows for algorithmic separation of these two groups of users[41]. Bot accounts in online debates also exhibited "always-on" behaviors, creating dense clusters of high-frequency posters that systematically amplified inflammatory content around the clock. In contrast, human-operated accounts fell into more diffuse, lower-frequency clusters and have more irregular, organic posting patterns[42].

A common clustering algorithm is the *k*-means clustering. This algorithm begins by selecting a *k* number of groups. This value *k* is typically analyst-defined. Then, the algorithm computes the centroids of those groups based on the chosen input features, i.e., posting frequency. A group centroid is the average position of all the accounts in that group across the selected feature vector, serving as the representative center of the cluster. Each account is assigned to the group whose centroid most closely matches its behavior, and the algorithm iteratively adjusts the centroids until the clusters stabilize. With posting frequency as input features, the *k*-means algorithm would typically yield one dense cluster of accounts posting at extremely high rates, and another cluster of accounts posting at more moderate rates. The former high-volume group of accounts, characterized by the intensity and regularity of posting frequency, is more likely to be Bots, while the low-volume group is more likely to represent human behavior.

Frequency is also an important metric in the detection of coordinated behavior. When multiple accounts exhibit unusually synchronized posting rates, this may indicate groups of organized Bots working together to flood the platform with content at scale[43]. The process of identification of

---

[40] Li, Linda, Orsolya Vásárhelyi, and Balázs Vedres. "Social bots spoil activist sentiment without eroding engagement." *Scientific Reports* 14, no. 1 (2024): 27005.
[41] Chu, Zi, Steven Gianvecchio, Haining Wang, and Sushil Jajodia. "Detecting automation of twitter accounts: Are you a human, bot, or cyborg?." *IEEE Transactions on dependable and secure computing* 9, no. 6 (2012): 811-824.
[42] Shao, Chengcheng, Giovanni Luca Ciampaglia, Onur Varol, Kai-Cheng Yang, Alessandro Flammini, and Filippo Menczer. "The spread of low-credibility content by social bots." *Nature communications* 9, no. 1 (2018): 4787.
[43] Magelinski, Thomas, Lynnette Ng, and Kathleen Carley. "A synchronized action framework for detection of coordination on social media." *Journal of Online Trust and Safety* 1, no. 2 (2022). ; Graham, Timothy, Sam Hames, and Elizabeth Alpert.

coordination is described in Chapter 4 “Coordinated Interactions”. Clustering groups of users by their coordinated behavior highlights not only individual automation but the collective patterns of orchestrated influence campaigns.

Clustering through temporal spikes. The timing of posting activity provides another powerful signal for clustering. Temporal spikes occur when groups of accounts show sudden surges in activity within the same narrow time window. Human posting is generally irregular and individualistic, so sharp bursts of activity by a group of accounts suggests an automatic reaction to a trigger. This trigger can be temporally based, (i.e., a group of accounts posts every Sunday), or event based (i..e, a group of account always reacts to a soccer match), or topic based (i.e., a group of account posts when a certain politician is being discussed). Temporal clustering is a valuable complement to frequency-based clustering. While frequency highlights persistent differences in user activity, temporal spikes capture moments of organized and correlated surges.

Studies of Bot activities during political events provide strong evidence of this temporal clustering pattern which can be used to differentiate Bots and humans. Bots often have periodic intervals between posts that result in bursty rhythms, producing activity streams that appear unnaturally regular or excessive as compared to the erratic posting behavior of humans. Such behavioral periodicity has been identified as a key signature of automation, since humans typically vary their online activity based on their circadian rhythms, their daily routines or contextual factors, whereas Bots can operate continuously with machine energy and precision[44].

In a study of 2019 Indonesian discourse, Bots have been observed to maintain low levels of activity throughout most of the year, but sharply increase their posting around periods of national and regional elections,

---

"The coordination network toolkit: a framework for detecting and analysing coordinated behaviour on social media." Journal of Computational Social Science 7, no. 2 (2024): 1139-1160.

[44] Gleasure, Rob, Maylis Saigot, and Irfan Kanat. "Let’s Talk About It in the Morning: How Circadian Rhythms Impact Information Sharing on Social Media." *Affective Science* 5, no. 4 (2024): 389-404. ; Hayawi, Kadhim, Susmita Saha, Mohammad Mehedy Masud, Sujith Samuel Mathew, and Mohammed Kaosar. "Social media bot detection with deep learning methods: a systematic review." *Neural Computing and Applications* 35, no. 12 (2023): 8903-8918.

sustaining elevated activity only for the duration of campaign[45]. Other observations have described a "waterfall pattern", where Bot accounts alternate between slow, steady drips of activity and sudden massive bursts upon triggered[46]. These empirical data show that temporal spikes can be used as a robust signal of Bot activity across diverse sociopolitical settings.

Clustering is a multi-dimensional problem. Accounts can exhibit multiple properties simultaneously, which means a single account may appear to belong to more than one cluster, depending on the set of features considered for the algorithm. For example, an account may resemble a Bot in its posting frequency but appear more human-like in its interaction diversity. As such, it requires analytic judgment to discern which set of features and type of cluster makes sense for the research question at hand, and for identifying the desired Bot behavior. This judgement can be made by considering the event being analyzed. For example, if the event is a one-off event such as a few months of heightened political activity, clustering by frequency of posting and frequency of coordinated actions is suitable. If the event were over a long period of time, with multiple sub-narratives, clustering by temporal spikes is more suitable. Such an event could be the analysis of Bot activity surrounding a soccer team, in which temporal spikes would be expected on the days that the team plays at home.

Each method of clustering illuminates different facets of account behavior. A frequency-based clustering highlights high-volume Bot accounts, while a temporal-based clustering uncovers synchronized spikes of activities. Employing these different clustering solutions underscores that Bot detection is not a single surfaced problem, and each perspective provides an additional layer of analysis for understanding how automated accounts behave in context.

One way to systematically integrate these perspectives is through a method called multi-view clustering. Multi-view clustering combines different views of the data, such as temporal activity, content similarity, and network

---

[45] Danaditya, Adya, Lynnette Hui Xian Ng, and Kathleen M. Carley. "From curious hashtags to polarized effect: profiling coordinated actions in indonesian twitter discourse." *Social Network Analysis and Mining* 12, no. 1 (2022): 105.

[46] Mazza, Michele, Stefano Cresci, Marco Avvenuti, Walter Quattrociocchi, and Maurizio Tesconi. "Rtbust: Exploiting temporal patterns for botnet detection on twitter." In *Proceedings of the 10th ACM conference on web science*, pp. 183-192. 2019.

connections into a unified clustering outcome[47]. This algorithm is particularly well-suited for social-based data, because it accounts for high inter-view and intra-view variability that single-view approaches do not handle. This algorithm has been applied with empirical robustness and scalability across diverse, large-scale social datasets. The algorithm is a module from the ORA-Pro software[48].

The multi-view clustering technique was applied to the 2020 coronavirus pandemic to analyze online discourse of four distinct views of X activity[49]: the text of tweets, the hashtags used in the tweets, the URLs that co-occurred with those hashtags, and the co-occurrence patterns of those hashtags within the tweets. When clustered around multiple feature spaces simultaneously, accounts that appeared normal when examined through a single view could form dense clusters when their combined behaviors were considered. One example is topical groups that directed the coronavirus discussion to topics like the Syrian civil war or the protests in Hong Kong. From only the hashtag view, these groups do not surface, but when examined through the text, hashtag and co-occurrence of hashtags views, these groups pop out. By synthesizing multiple behavioral dimensions, the multi-view clustering technique offers a more comprehensive lens for identifying Bot activity and influence operations.

Bot Networks

Bot networks, also known as **BotNets**, are clusters of Bots that operate collectively towards common goals. Bot accounts do not necessarily work in isolation and can team up with other Bots to amplify their effects, making their collective work more powerful than single accounts acting alone [50]. These goals can be to disseminate a single narrative, to boost the visibility

---

[47] Cruickshank, Iain J. "Multi-view clustering of social-based data." (2020). PhD Thesis, Carnegie Mellon University.

[48] https://netanomics.com/ora-pro/

[49] Cruickshank, Iain J. "Multi-view clustering of social-based data." (2020). PhD Thesis, Carnegie Mellon University.

[50] Khaund, Tuja, Baris Kirdemir, Nitin Agarwal, Huan Liu, and Fred Morstatter. "Social bots and their coordination during online campaigns: a survey." *IEEE Transactions on Computational Social Systems* 9, no. 2 (2021): 530-545.

of specific hashtags, or to artificially prop up the influence of targeted accounts[51].

In 2017, about 13,000 Bot-like X accounts were part of a Bot network that attempted to sway the result of the UK Brexit referendum[52]. This BotNet operated to amplify the "Leave" campaign that advocated for the United Kingdom to leave the European Union. These Bots were identified by inspecting URLs and domain-sharing patterns, which revealed clusters of accounts posting links from Bot-controlled sites. The BotNet displayed clear specialization: some accounts repeatedly shared campaign slogans, others focused on distributing URLs, and even others amplified posts by seed users to trigger discussion cascades. Interestingly, this BotNet was highly active in the run up to the referendum, but disappeared quickly shortly after the ballot was casted, suggesting that its purpose was tied to influencing the vote outcome.

Another example is the Syrian BotNet that was active on X during the 2012 Syrian civil war. This network operated for more than six months and primarily circulated political opinions and cartoons[53]. Structurally, this BotNet exhibited a core-periphery pattern. A small core of Bots generated large volumes of original tweets of the order of about 1,600 tweets per week. The peripheral Bots retweeted and amplified those tweets, distributing political ideology throughout X.

The same core-periphery network architecture appeared in the 2022 online discourse surrounding US House Speaker Nancy Pelosi's visit to Taiwan. Roughly 11,000 accounts participated in a BotNet[54]. The core Bots launched a campaign asserting that Taiwan is part of China. Peripheral Bots

---

[51] Ng, Lynnette HX, and Araz Taeihagh. "How does fake news spread? Understanding pathways of disinformation spread through APIs." *Policy & Internet* 13, no. 4 (2021): 560-585.

[52] Bastos, Marco T., and Dan Mercea. "The Brexit botnet and user-generated hyperpartisan news." *Social science computer review* 37, no. 1 (2019): 38-54.

[53] Abokhodair, Norah, Daisy Yoo, and David W. McDonald. "Dissecting a social botnet: Growth, content and influence in Twitter." In *Proceedings of the 18th ACM conference on computer supported cooperative work & social computing*, pp. 839-851. 2015.

[54] Jacobs, Charity S., Lynnette Hui Xian Ng, and Kathleen M. Carley. "Tracking china's cross-strait bot networks against taiwan." In *International conference on social computing, behavioral-cultural modeling and prediction and behavior representation in modeling and simulation*, pp. 115-125. Cham: Springer Nature Switzerland, 2023.

replicated the content through retweets and copy-paste tactics. Such a structured allowed the wide propagation of the desired narrative through the social network.

In the Syrian and the Taiwan scenarios, the Bots exploited the illusory truth effect. The illusory truth effect is a cognitive bias where repeated exposure to the same message increases its perceived validity[55]. By flooding social media feeds with identical slogans, links, and cartoons, the BotNets familiarize their audiences with the narratives. Over time, this familiarity of narratives makes them more believable, regardless of their source or factual accuracy[56]. This effect has been also researched to increase consumer belief in misinformation[57]. In both our examples, the combined and sustained effort of the BotNets served to promote strategic geopolitical narratives.

While individual Bots can sometimes evade detection whether through false negatives from the Bot detection algorithm or through the clever human mimicry of the Bot design, their collective behavior within a BotNet is harder to conceal. BotNet detection often relies on a clustering algorithm. For example, a BotNet can be identified through clustering groups of accounts that use the same hashtags, or retweet the same content or follow highly similar posting schedules[58]. By focusing on these group-level dynamics rather than constructing feature sets of the individual behaviors, analysts can identify accounts with Bot-like behavior that would otherwise slip through the cracks.

Importantly, not all BotNets are harmful. There are BotNets that serve constructive purposes, such as to disseminate information. The Australian

---

[55] Udry, Jessica, and Sarah J. Barber. "The illusory truth effect: A review of how repetition increases belief in misinformation." *Current Opinion in Psychology* 56 (2024): 101736.
[56] Roggeveen, Anne L., and Gita Venkataramani Johar. "Perceived source variability versus familiarity: Testing competing explanations for the truth effect." *Journal of Consumer Psychology* 12, no. 2 (2002): 81-91.
[57] Vellani, Valentina, Sarah Zheng, Dilay Ercelik, and Tali Sharot. "The illusory truth effect leads to the spread of misinformation." *Cognition* 236 (2023): 105421.
[58] Keller, Tobias R., and Ulrike Klinger. "Social bots in election campaigns: Theoretical, empirical, and methodological implications." *Political Communication* 36, no. 1 (2019): 171-189. ; Pacheco, Diogo, Pik-Mai Hui, Christopher Torres-Lugo, Bao Tran Truong, Alessandro Flammini, and Filippo Menczer. "Uncovering coordinated networks on social media: methods and case studies." In *Proceedings of the international AAAI conference on web and social media*, vol. 15, pp. 455-466. 2021.

news organization 7News manages multiple state-level X accounts that post synchronized updates within seconds of each other[59], particularly during national emergencies such as the 2020 coronavirus pandemic. This BotNet used networked automation to disseminate vital information across different local audiences, and ensure timely and consistent communication of the then-fast evolving social and health policies and updates.

Responsible Use of Bot Detectors

Bot detection algorithms can be powerful, but their application carries some risks. We discuss three points on how Bot detection algorithms can be used responsibly: understanding the risks of false positives, the implications of labeling users, and the importance of transparency in automated classification.

Dealing with false positives. A central challenge is the risk in false positives, where legitimate human users are mislabeled as Bots. This problem can arise from the training data used, and therefore, a diverse set of training data is required to prevent out of domain errors. Out-of-domain errors occur when the algorithm simply labels the account as a Bot or human because it has not seen it before[60].

Responsible probability thresholding. This problem can also evolve from the probability threshold used for classifying accounts into Bots or humans. A threshold that is too loose means a lower P(bot) score is required for the account to be classified as a Bot, which can result in too many false positives. A threshold that is too tight means the account features must match close to the training data to be considered a Bot. The bot probability threshold value is a decimal value between 0 and 1. What a threshold of 0.50 means is that the algorithm has determined that the number of bot-like features that a user has is greater than the average number of bot features. Humans can also exhibit bot-like features, so classifying a user as a bot when it's P(bot) score is above a threshold does not guarantee that it is a bot, but it indicates the degree the user's features match that of known bots.

---

[59] Magelinski, Thomas, Lynnette Ng, and Kathleen Carley. "A synchronized action framework for detection of coordination on social media." *Journal of Online Trust and Safety* 1, no. 2 (2022).

[60] Echeverra, Juan, Emiliano De Cristofaro, Nicolas Kourtellis, Ilias Leontiadis, Gianluca Stringhini, and Shi Zhou. "LOBO: Evaluation of generalization deficiencies in Twitter bot classifiers." In *Proceedings of the 34th annual computer security applications conference*, pp. 137-146. 2018.

By going with a higher threshold (e.g., 0.8), we indicate that we want to be very sure that the user matches a lot of bot-like features.

Throughout the literature, many threshold values have been used, even for the same algorithm. For example, for the Botometer algorithm, a study on the spread of low-credibility content in 2016 data used the threshold of 0.50[61], while studies on nicotine-related discussions used a threshold of 0.80[62]. One way to reduce the false positives is to systematically determine a stable threshold through a longitudinal analysis. Such an analysis involves applying a Bot detection algorithm across a large number of agents and scoring Bot classification time slice by time slice. The threshold would be one that results in a stable Bot classification, where there are minimal changes of the threshold value across all agents over time. This method has been performed on the existing BotBuster and BotHunter algorithms[63]. Such thresholding experiments show that a 0.70 score is a good cut off to reliably and consistently differentiate bot and human users.

Implications of labeling a user. The implications of labeling users as Bots also demand careful attention. There are many Reddit posts where users are seeking help from being labeled as a Bot, whether on Reddit or other social media platforms. These users call out as, "Guys, They keep thinking that I'm a Bot! Help!"[64], "Why do I keep getting labeled as a bot whenever I post???"[65], "Reddit thinks I'm a bot. I'm not a bot. I'm a hooman"[66].

---

[61] Shao, Chengcheng, Giovanni Luca Ciampaglia, Onur Varol, Kai-Cheng Yang, Alessandro Flammini, and Filippo Menczer. "The spread of low-credibility content by social bots." *Nature communications* 9, no. 1 (2018): 4787.

[62] Allem, Jon-Patrick, Allison Dormanesh, Anuja Majmundar, Jennifer B. Unger, Matthew G. Kirkpatrick, Akshat Choube, Aneesh Aithal, Emilio Ferrara, and Tess Boley Cruz. "Topics of nicotine-related discussions on Twitter: infoveillance study." *Journal of medical Internet research* 23, no. 6 (2021): e25579.

[63] Ng, Lynnette Hui Xian, and Kathleen M. Carley. "Botbuster: Multi-platform bot detection using a mixture of experts." In *Proceedings of the international AAAI conference on web and social media*, vol. 17, pp. 686-697. 2023. ; Ng, Lynnette Hui Xian, Dawn C. Robertson, and Kathleen M. Carley. "Stabilizing a supervised bot detection algorithm: How much data is needed for consistent predictions?." *Online Social Networks and Media* 28 (2022): 100198.

[64] https://www.reddit.com/r/HomeNetworking/comments/qj7vpb/guys_they_keep_thinking_that_im_a_bot_help/

[65] https://www.reddit.com/r/NewToReddit/comments/179hsqd/why_do_i_keep_getting_labeled_as_a_bot_whenever_i/

[66] https://www.reddit.com/r/bugs/comments/z1qoau/reddit_thinks_im_a_bot_im_not_a_bot_im_a_hooman/

Labeling a human account as a Bot can be viewed as a defamation of their character. This can lead to cyber-bullying where other accounts jeer at the mislabeled account, or falsely report the mislabeled account as if the account were a real Bot. This reduces the human user's experience on the social media platform, or results in the user's suspension from the platform. Such Bot accusations were weaponized in politically sensitive contexts[67].

One must understand that when Bot detection algorithms mark a user as a Bot, it is not necessarily guaranteed to be a Bot. Rather, the algorithm guarantees that the account has many characteristics that are common to known Bots. Instead of a sweeping generalization that a Bot is bad, analysts should first identify the account's behavior and identity before making a conclusion of its malice. For example, a Bot that simply posts the time at regular intervals does not do harm to the online ecosystem, but a Bot that regularly posts extremist messages does. In Chapter 3, we will present that Bots exist on a spectrum of goodness, and in Chapter 6, we will present a typology of Bot personas. These are tools which can be used to evaluate the Bot's harm on the digital ecosystem.

Transparency of Bot detection algorithms. Finally, the transparency of the Bot detection algorithms is another key consideration. Bot detection models often rely on opaque machine learning techniques such as deep neural networks, which may achieve high accuracy but offer limited interpretability. Moving forward, Bot detection algorithms should reveal the features that contribute to the account's Bot label, by using techniques that analyze the algorithm's working. For example, Bot detectors that use random forests can use the mean decrease in impurity to identify important features. One such study determined that the entropy of the screenname and username and the retweet and like count of a post are the most important features in Bot determination[68]. Tools like Botometer also provide nuanced

---

[67] "How Americans Wound Up on Twitter's List of Russian Bots." *WIRED*, July 20, 2018. https://www.wired.com/story/how-americans-wound-up-on-twitters-list-of-russian-bots/ ; "Twitter Pulls Plug on @OscarsAudioGuy Spoof Account." *WIRED*, February 27, 2012. https://www.wired.com/2012/02/oscars-audio-guy-banned/

[68] Ng, Lynnette Hui Xian, and Kathleen M. Carley. "Assembling a multi-platform ensemble social bot detector with applications to us 2020 elections." *Social Network Analysis and Mining* 14, no. 1 (2024): 45.

breakdown of features like the friendship network, the user metadata, the sentiment of content, that the Bot score is based on [69].

Responsible use of Bot detectors requires balancing accuracy with ethical safeguards, such that humans can harness automation for social good, yet malicious users are properly detected and weeded out. Therefore, it is important to recognize that simply classifying an account as a Bot is insufficient for a well-rounded analysis and dimensions of goodness and Bot personas should also be considered.

---

[69] Yang, Kai-Cheng, Emilio Ferrara, and Filippo Menczer. "Botometer 101: Social bot practicum for computational social scientists." *Journal of computational social science* 5, no. 2 (2022): 1511-1528.

3

THE SOCIAL ASPECT OF BOTS

Public opinion often paints social media Bots in dark colors. They are seen as the invisible architects of chaos—spreading conspiracy theories during elections or amplifying outrage after every controversial headline. According to a Pew Research Center survey, nearly 80 percent of Americans familiar with Bots believe they are mostly harmful[70]. Yet this perception tells only half the story. Not all Bots are digital villains. Some track wildfires in real time, alerting residents before danger spreads. Others answer routine customer queries so human support teams can focus on complex needs. Community forums even rely on moderation bots to flag hate speech and maintain civility. In short, bots are not inherently bad. They reflect the intentions of those who design and deploy them.

Another dimension along which bots vary is visibility. Some Bots step into the light, proudly labeling themselves as automated helpers. For example, X has introduced a feature that allows accounts to display a "bot" tag, highlighting bots that serve clear public good, such as those posting earthquake warnings or updating followers on vaccination appointments. These overt Bots choose transparency, building trust by waving their artificial flag for all to see. In stark contrast, covert Bots slip through the digital crowd wearing human masks: they craft elaborate fake personas, mimic authentic conversations, and blend in so seamlessly that even savvy users are often fooled. Deceptive Bots might join heated political debates or pose as helpful commentators, weaving misinformation into the public discourse while hiding their true nature. This spectrum of the radically transparent to the relentlessly deceptive Bot agent underscores the urgent challenge of distinguishing honest automation from digital masquerade.

Bots span a spectrum of goodness and visibility, from helpful and transparent to harmful and deceptive. This chapter helps readers appreciate

---

[70] https://www.pewresearch.org/journalism/2018/10/15/social-media-bots-draw-publics-attention-and-concern/

this spectrum, showing how Bots can be both allies and adversaries in online spaces, and examines the challenges that researchers face in studying them.

A Spectrum of Bot Goodness and Visibility

A knife can be used to chop vegetables, or it can be used to kill someone. The knife is neither good nor bad; it is the person who wields the knife that can make its employment good or bad. Likewise, the computer technology that is used to program a Bot is neutral. However, unlike knives, Bots have increasingly evolved from simple automation scripts to actors with agency in the digital ecosystem. When Bots possess agency, they can make autonomous choices — such as generating content, responding to users, or even forming relationships —without direct human intervention. This power allows bots to impact conversations and influence outcomes on social media, sometimes acting according to their own programmed goals rather than simply following basic commands. While their code still originates from human design, Bots can operate with a degree of autonomy to make decisions about when, how and to whom, to deliver content and interact with. In some cases, their programming allows for adaptation through supervised learning or reinforcement learning.

Bots therefore cannot be understood as merely passive tools, but are in fact, sociotechnical agents embedded within human networks[71]. Regulation that assumes Bots are only tools will fail to capture their evolving role as influential digital actors[72]. Bots are not only instruments of their human creators, but are also participants in the digital ecosystems, capable of shaping discourse, reinforcing biases and sustaining influence operations. Recognizing this agency is crucial for developing governance mechanisms that cope with such a landscape of digital agents.

A Bot's ethical positioning exists on a spectrum, from highly beneficial to human society to deeply harmful, depending on how its capabilities are directed and expressed. Where a Bot lies on the spectrum is dependent on how human operators choose to employ it, but also how the Bot evolves.

---

[71] Riedl, Martin J. "Negotiating sociomateriality and commensurability: Human and algorithmic editorial judgment at social media platforms." *Journalism Studies* 23, no. 3 (2022): 374-391. ; Carley, Kathleen M. "Computational organization science: A new frontier." *Proceedings of the National Academy of Sciences* 99, no. suppl_3 (2002): 7257-7262.

[72] Woolley, Samuel C. "Automating power: Social bot interference in global politics." *First Monday* (2016).

Microsoft's Tay Bot was initially built to have conversations casual and friendly conversations with users on Twitter, but through repeated interactions with users, this Bot quickly learned and reproduced toxic language patterns[73]. Within just sixteen hours of its launch, Tay had to be suspended because it generated racist and inflammatory tweets and used offensive content. Tay is an example of how as much as humans are influenced by Bots, Bots are also influenced by humans and they learn from human society.

The goodness of a Bot only tells one part of the story. Equally important about a Bot is its visibility. By visibility, we mean how overtly the Bot declares its automated nature. A Bot sits on a spectrum of overtness, from where it openly declares that it is automated, to the other covert end, where it manipulates opinions under the cloak of anonymity.

When the two spectra are combined – goodness on one axis and visibility on another axis – they form a quadrant framework for understanding Bots. **Figure 3.1** illustrates the four quadrants of Bot goodness and visibility and lists some examples of types of Bots that fall within each quadrant.

Some Bots will always fall squarely in one quadrant. These Bots are non-reactive and non-adaptive towards other users and the social narratives and therefore will always have the same functionality across their life span. Such Bots are typically software programs that perform a few tasks. For example, the *BigBenBot* is a Bot on X that tweets out the time every hour like a clockwork.

Other Bots adapt and do not fall squarely within one quadrant or another, nor do they remain fixed in a single quadrant over their life span. The most obvious quadrant move happens when good Bots are hijacked for bad intent, as was observed during a 2021 protest about Kashmir where food-related accounts were transformed into accounts promoting uprising for freedom[74]. These Bots were initially posting photos of mouth-watering food and recommending them, before they were taken over during the 2021 Kashmir

---

[73] Neff, Gina. "Talking to bots: Symbiotic agency and the case of Tay." *International journal of Communication* (2016).

[74] Ng, Lynnette Hui Xian, and Kathleen M. Carley. "Bot-based emotion behavior differences in images during Kashmir black day event." In *International Conference on Social Computing, Behavioral-Cultural Modeling and Prediction and Behavior Representation in Modeling and Simulation*, pp. 184-194. Cham: Springer International Publishing, 2021.

Black Day event. The Kashmir Black day event is an annual day of protest observed by the separatists and activist groups to denounce the Indian government in the Kashmir region and call for independence. During the 2021 iteration, these Bots posted a series of tweets that called other users to join the protest for freedom.

Similarly, covert Bots that spread religious and political ideologies during key Indonesian events appear benign when they are dormant but are malicious when they are active[75]. These Bots "sleep" for most of the time, and do not post any content nor interact online. They wake up when there are religious debates such as the debate about the prohibition of alcoholic beverages, and impact the intensity of the debate to promote narratives of a religious and Islamic state. Such was an example of how Bots can be used to make it seem like there is an overwhelming consensus when there is actually none, and vice-versa.

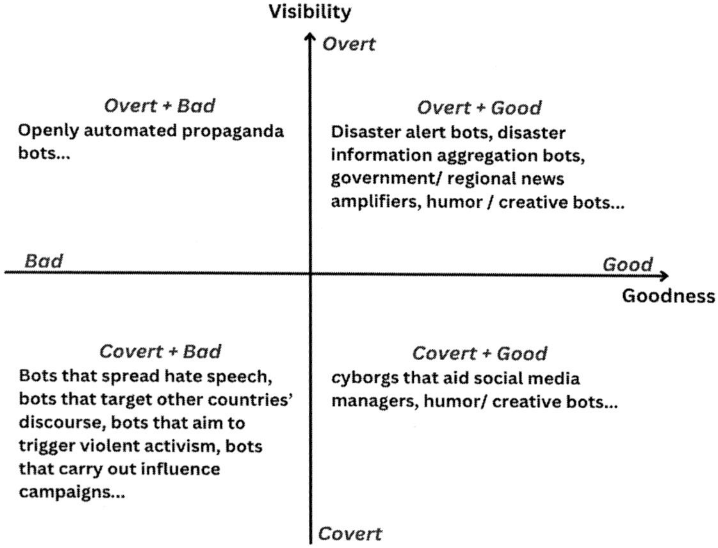

Figure 3.1: Quadrant framework of Bot goodness and visibility

[75] Danaditya, Adya, Lynnette Hui Xian Ng, and Kathleen M. Carley. "From curious hashtags to polarized effect: profiling coordinated actions in indonesian twitter discourse." *Social Network Analysis and Mining* 12, no. 1 (2022): 105.

Overt Bots stride onto social media with absolute candor. Their automated nature is emblazoned on their profiles, often with "bot" right in their usernames or an official label announcing them as automated accounts. On X, for example, overt bots like Thread Reader App unroll long Twitter threads for users, while entertainment bots such as Dank Memer on Discord openly fill chats with jokes and memes. GitHub hosts many overt bots that openly declare their automated status, often through their profile names or project descriptions. Examples include Bots like AllContributors, which publicly adds credits to project documentation, Dependabot, which automatically updates dependencies, and CodeCov, which transparently reports code coverage on pull requests. These bots are celebrated for handling repetitive tasks and improving project workflows, making their automation visible and beneficial to all users involved. These transparent bots serve the public directly: they break news, entertain, answer questions, do repetitive tasks, or keep digital communities running smoothly, making no attempt to masquerade as human. Overt bots embrace their role as digital tools, signaling that not every automated presence online is hiding in the shadows.

Covert Bots operate behind digital masks, concealing their true nature as they impersonate real humans and weave themselves into online communities. Their survival depends on deception: these bots craft detailed personas, mimic human speech patterns, and even mirror the interests and behaviors of actual users, all to avoid detection. A striking example is the Russian bot farm exposed in 2024, where AI-powered bots created thousands of realistic American profiles across platforms, using fake photos and tailored bios to blend in and amplify divisive narratives. Covert bots are the hidden hands behind influence operations, their camouflaged presence making them powerful tools for manipulating opinion and distorting public discourse.

Good Bots aid human users and communities in their online activity. They spread good content and seek to promote positive emotions. Good Bots are used in many situations: e.g., to announce alerts on social media about impending earthquakes[76], to aggregate disparate social media information

[76] Avvenuti, Marco, Stefano Cresci, Andrea Marchetti, Carlo Meletti, and Maurizio Tesconi. "Ears (earthquake alert and report system) a real time decision support system for earthquake crisis management." In *Proceedings of the 20th ACM SIGKDD international conference on knowledge discovery and data mining*, pp. 1749-1758. 2014.

during disasters[77], to amplify government and regional news during crisis situations[78], to alleviate the workload of social media managers, politicians and influencers[79], to synchronously broadcast news from state accounts to region-specific accounts[80], and for humor and creative purposes[81]. Good Bots are often overt Bots.

Bad Bots do ill to the information ecosystem and disrupt the virtual space. Their activities have a negative effect on the social media ecosystem, which can sometimes spill over into the offline world, therefore making them the agent that researchers, businesses and governments are most concerned about. Bad Bots may be built by state-sponsored actors, and programmed with agendas that serve the actors' political or strategic objectives[82]. The operations of Bad Bots typically include: amplify politically divisive or socially stratified narratives or hate speech[83], seed and amplify narratives that target other countries[84], trigger and initiate activism[85], seed and create

---

[77] Crooks, Andrew, Arie Croitoru, Anthony Stefanidis, and Jacek Radzikowski. "# Earthquake: Twitter as a distributed sensor system." *Transactions in GIS* 17, no. 1 (2013): 124-147.

[78] Chang, Ho-Chun Herbert, and Emilio Ferrara. "Comparative analysis of social bots and humans during the COVID-19 pandemic." *Journal of Computational Social Science* 5, no. 2 (2022): 1409-1425.

[79] Ng, Lynnette Hui Xian, Dawn C. Robertson, and Kathleen M. Carley. "Cyborgs for strategic communication on social media." *Big Data & Society* 11, no. 1 (2024): 20539517241231275.

[80] Magelinski, Thomas, Lynnette Ng, and Kathleen Carley. "A synchronized action framework for detection of coordination on social media." *Journal of Online Trust and Safety* 1, no. 2 (2022).

[81] Aldayel, Abeer, and Walid Magdy. "Characterizing the role of bots' in polarized stance on social media." *Social Network Analysis and Mining* 12, no. 1 (2022): 30.

[82] Woolley, Samuel C. "Bots and computational propaganda: Automation for communication and control." *Social Media and Democracy: The State of the Field, Prospects for Reform. Cambridge* (2020): 89-110.

[83] Uyheng, Joshua, Daniele Bellutta, and Kathleen M. Carley. "Bots amplify and redirect hate speech in online discourse about racism during the COVID-19 pandemic." *Social Media+ Society* 8, no. 3 (2022): 20563051221104749.

[84] Jacobs, Charity S., Lynnette Hui Xian Ng, and Kathleen M. Carley. "Tracking china's cross-strait bot networks against taiwan." In *International conference on social computing, behavioral-cultural modeling and prediction and behavior representation in modeling and simulation*, pp. 115-125. Cham: Springer Nature Switzerland, 2023.

[85] Ng, Lynnette Hui Xian, and Kathleen M. Carley. "Bot-based emotion behavior differences in images during Kashmir black day event." In *International Conference on Social Computing, Behavioral-Cultural Modeling and Prediction and Behavior*

online politically-charged influence campaigns[86]. Bad Bots are often covert Bots.

Social media platforms or governing bodies (i.e., governments, think tanks) are not the only organizations that determine the goodness of a Bot. The virtual community can also provide indications on unacceptable qualities. For example, in the subreddit r/botrequests, automation ideas are sometimes responded to negatively by other users (i.e., "sounds like creeperbot", "that isn't very nice"). This "trial by audience" method can be useful to give analysts an idea of the Bot behaviors that are not socially accepted by online users, and are most often the same behaviors that human users perceive to be malicious[87].

Challenges of Social Media Bot Research

Social media Bot research can be intellectually exciting and societally important, but it faces constant challenges that complicate the reliability, comparability and interpretation of findings. We elaborate on three main challenges: data collection, Bot evolution and interpretation of Bot impact.

Data collection. Data for social media Bot research relies heavily on the ability to access and extract content from the social media platforms. However, the design and features of these platforms constantly change, as companies iterate to improve user experiences. New functionalities are continually being added while other features are deprecated. Changes in features means that researchers need to rework their data collection and processing pipelines. The disappearance of features mean that algorithms that make use of the feature cannot produce reliable results, and addition of features mean researchers should consider harnessing the feature to make better inferences from the data. Such feature changes also mean that the algorithms previously built for finding Bots may no longer work because of the reliance of a particular discontinued feature. This algorithmic deficiency

---

Representation in Modeling and Simulation, pp. 184-194. Cham: Springer International Publishing, 2021.

[86] Khaund, Tuja, Baris Kirdemir, Nitin Agarwal, Huan Liu, and Fred Morstatter. "Social bots and their coordination during online campaigns: a survey." *IEEE Transactions on Computational Social Systems* 9, no. 2 (2021): 530-545.

[87] Long, Kiel, John Vines, Selina Sutton, Phillip Brooker, Tom Feltwell, Ben Kirman, Julie Barnett, and Shaun Lawson. "" Could You Define That in Bot Terms"? Requesting, Creating and Using Bots on Reddit." In *Proceedings of the 2017 CHI Conference on Human Factors in Computing Systems*, pp. 3488-3500. 2017.

has been documented in leave-one-out experiments that show how missing features can decrease the accuracy of Bot detection algorithms built with supervised machine learning techniques[88].

Another barrier is data unavailability. Some platforms provide APIs, or Application Programming Interfaces, to allow researchers to collect data from their site. However, these APIs may be restricted by paywalls, access tiers or rate limits, that limit the scale data researchers can feasibly collect. A recent example is the shift of X's API to a paid model in 2023, which costed $200 a month for the basic tier, reducing the ability of many researchers without financial backing to access large-scale datasets[89]. In a similar fashion, Reddit moved from a free API access to a paid version in June 2023. This move caused many small companies that relied on the API access to close out of business[90]. Other platforms do not provide APIs, and researchers must decide how to ethically collect the data, whether via automated web scraping, manual download, or surveying respondents to provide their data.

Finally, data in the form of deleted or suspended posts or accounts are usually not available as post-hoc data to researchers. Another type of inaccessible data is data where users have changed their privacy settings to restrict their posts from public view. Over time, social media users have grown more privacy conscious. Their trust in platforms declined, have an increased perception of online risk, and are less willing to disclose personal information[91]. Such changes in privacy settings leave researchers unable to determine if the user is a Bot, or analyze the community the user belongs to,

---

88 Echeverra, Juan, Emiliano De Cristofaro, Nicolas Kourtellis, Ilias Leontiadis, Gianluca Stringhini, and Shi Zhou. "LOBO: Evaluation of generalization deficiencies in Twitter bot classifiers." In *Proceedings of the 34th annual computer security applications conference*, pp. 137-146. 2018.

89 Sarah Grevy Gotfredsen, "What Happened to Academic Research on Twitter?" *Columbia Journalism Review*, December 6, 2023, https://www.cjr.org/tow_center/qa-what-happened-to-academic-research-on-twitter.php ; Chris Stokel-Walker, "Twitter's $42,000-per-Month API Prices Out Nearly Everyone," *Wired*, February 2023, https://www.wired.com/story/twitter-data-api-prices-out-nearly-everyone/

90 https://en.wikipedia.org/wiki/Reddit_API_controversy

91 Boyd, Danah. "Social network sites as networked publics: Affordances, dynamics, and implications." In *A networked self*, pp. 47-66. Routledge, 2010. ; Alwahaishi, Saleh, Mohammad Saad Al-Ahmadi, Zulqurnain Ali, and Ibrahim Al-Jabri. "Self-Disclosure on Social Media: Do Personality Traits Matter?." *Sage Open* 14, no. 2 (2024): 21582440241255754.

or the participation of the user within the online discourse. Such missing data and changes or user privacy settings can leave important discussions of historical events unobservable.

To mitigate these limitations, researchers can diversify their data sources and collection methods, combining official APIs with ethically designed web scraping (in accordance to the platform's rules and regulations), or collaborating with third-party archives and organizations.

Bot Evolution. Bots are not static agents. They adapt their behavioral signatures, often in response to the changes in platform affordances and technology evolution. Changes in platform features mean that Bot detection algorithms must be constantly trained to adapt to the new datasets, where features that are no longer useful are not considered, while newer features are integrated[92]. The evolution of Bots can be seen in the content they post. Expert-curated datasets of Twitter Bots from 2016 wrote with simpler linguistic forms, whereas Bots from 2020 exhibit increasingly sophisticated vocabularies[93], and Bots from 2024 have begun to use generative-AI models that construct very human-like sentences[94]. This shift complicates Bot identification not only algorithmically but also socially. In a study that asked 297 users to classify Bots across seven social networks, participants misclassified around half of the accounts they evaluated[95]. Modern Bots are designed to mimic human qualities that human assessors are constantly duped by them[96].

Researchers must adapt to the changing landscape by first continually retraining Bot detection models using recent data to capture emerging behaviors. Further, employing an ensemble of methods from machine

---

[92] Dhruv Mehrotra and Andrew Couts, "Bot Hunting Is All About the Vibes," *Wired*, September 30, 2022, https://www.wired.com/story/bot-hunting-is-all-about-the-vibes/.

[93] Ng, Lynnette Hui Xian, and Kathleen M. Carley. "Botbuster: Multi-platform bot detection using a mixture of experts." In *Proceedings of the international AAAI conference on web and social media*, vol. 17, pp. 686-697. 2023.

[94] Yang, Kai-Cheng, and Filippo Menczer. "Anatomy of an AI-powered malicious social botnet." *Journal of Quantitative Description: Digital Media* 4 (2024).

[95] Kats, Daniel, and Mahmood Sharif. ""I Have No Idea What a Social Bot Is": On Users' Perceptions of Social Bots and Ability to Detect Them." In *Proceedings of the 10th International Conference on Human-Agent Interaction*, pp. 32-40. 2022.

[96] Kenny, Ryan, Baruch Fischhoff, Alex Davis, Kathleen M. Carley, and Casey Canfield. "Duped by bots: why some are better than others at detecting fake social media personas." *Human factors* 66, no. 1 (2024): 88-102.

learning to statistical analysis to synchronization analyses can improve the accuracy of detection of such sophisticated Bots. We describe these methods in Sections 5 and 6.

Interpretation of impact. Even when Bots are successfully detected and characterized, measuring their actual influence can present a methodological challenge. High activity levels characteristic of Bots like frequent postings or content amplification do not necessarily equate to measurable changes in public opinion, or offline behaviors. In fact, some activity like the constant retweeting might reduce audience engagement, while other subtle signals like the use of emotions will increase engagement[97]. Visibility metrics commonly used in social media analytics like engagement counts (i.e., number of likes, retweets) reflect interaction at a snapshot in time but are often poor proxies for actual behavioral changes[98].

The mechanics of information spread on social media also deepens the complexity. Bots do not exist in isolation; they interact with humans and other Bots. Bot messages are often taken up, modified and shared or re-broadcasted by humans[99], making it difficult to disentangle automated influence from organic amplification. Information diffusion dynamics combined with network effects can artificially inflate the perceived prevalence and impact of the original Bot activity[100].

---

[97] Ng, Lynnette Hui Xian, Wenqi Zhou, and Kathleen M. Carley. "Exploring cognitive bias triggers in covid-19 misinformation tweets: A bot vs. human perspective." *arXiv preprint arXiv:2406.07293* (2024).

[98] Avram, Mihai, Nicholas Micallef, Sameer Patil, and Filippo Menczer. *"Exposure to Social Engagement Metrics Increases Vulnerability to Misinformation." Harvard Kennedy School Misinformation Review*, 2020.
https://misinforeview.hks.harvard.edu/article/exposure-to-social-engagement-metrics-increases-vulnerability-to-misinformation/; Ng, Lynnette Hui Xian; Zhou, Wenqi; Carley, Kathleen M. "Appeal and Scope of Misinformation Spread by AI Agents and Humans" Proceedings of the Americas Conference on Information Systems (AMCIS), 2025, Paper No. 6.

[99] Ng, Lynnette Hui Xian, Ian Kloo, Samantha Clark, and Kathleen M. Carley. "An exploratory analysis of COVID bot vs human disinformation dissemination stemming from the Disinformation Dozen on Telegram." *Journal of Computational Social Science* 7, no. 1 (2024): 695-720.

[100] Arif, Ahmer, Kelley Shanahan, Fang-Ju Chou, Yoanna Dosouto, Kate Starbird, and Emma S. Spiro. "How information snowballs: Exploring the role of exposure in

To improve interpretation, researchers should integrate multiple modes of analysis: combining quantitative computational, network and statistical analysis with qualitative content and historical analysis, to achieve a richer understanding of both scale and substance. Longitudinal time-series analyses will aid in measuring how Bots shape discourse over time.

Bot analysis is challenging. In social media bot analysis, the challenge begins with data collection and processing, which is constrained by platform APIs and constantly impacted by their evolving features. Even after building machine learning models or heuristics to detect bots, these defenses can quickly lose effectiveness because Bots rapidly evolve alongside changes in technology and user behavior. To maintain efficacy, Bot detectors must be updated continuously or at least on a frequent, near real-time basis to keep up with the accelerating sophistication of Bots. Despite updating detection systems, interpreting the impact of bots within the complex social media ecosystem remains an ongoing challenge, as bots increasingly mimic human behavior and blend seamlessly into online interactions. This necessitates not just updating detection tools regularly but also adapting strategies to the dynamic bot landscape for meaningful analysis and mitigation.

The social media ecosystem is evolving, and so too are the Bots. Indeed, many Bots can still be found with old techniques. Indicators that differentiate evolving bots from legacy Bots center on their sophistication, behavioral patterns, and technical capabilities. Legacy Bots typically adhere to older, rule-based methods characterized by uniform and repetitive activities such as repeatedly accessing the same URLs, limited interaction variety, and predictable timing lacking adaptability. They generally cannot replicate nuanced human-like behaviors such as variable mouse movements, diverse typing rhythms, or complex engagement with page elements. In contrast, the newer age Bots have evolved to employ cutting-edge techniques including scriptable headless browsers, AI-driven behavioral mimicry, and sophisticated session management that enable prolonged interactions and more effective evasion of basic detection. These Bots imitate natural user behavior through inconsistent mouse movements, varying typing speeds, and dynamic interaction durations, making them difficult to distinguish from human users. Furthermore, evolving Bots often possess real-time self-correction and adaptive capabilities to counteract defense mechanisms, features absent in legacy bots. Additional

---

online rumor propagation." In *Proceedings of the 19th ACM Conference on Computer-Supported Cooperative Work & Social Computing*, pp. 466-477. 2016.

distinguishing indicators include the ability to execute JavaScript, maintain session cookies, and interact dynamically with webpage elements, in contrast to the more static and predictable operations of legacy Bots.

Another factor that makes analysis difficult is that humans sometimes choose to emulate Bots. Humans imitate Bots in social media contexts primarily to manipulate online interactions, amplify messages, or engage in coordinated campaigns. Research from the University of Southern California and the University of Oxford highlights that social bots mimic human attributes to blend in, leveraging language and behavioral patterns to appear authentic[101]. This can encourage humans to interact with these accounts under false pretenses. In some scenarios, humans deliberately adopt Bot-like behaviors, such as repetitive posting or flooding networks, to simulate influence or control narratives. This strategy blurs the line between human and Bot behaviors, complicating detection efforts and amplifying misinformation or polarized content online.

[101] Ferrara, Emilio, Onur Varol, Clayton Davis, Filippo Menczer, and Alessandro Flammini. "The rise of social bots." *Communications of the ACM* 59, no. 7 (2016): 96-104. ; Woolley, Samuel C., and Philip N. Howard, eds. *Computational propaganda: Political parties, politicians, and political manipulation on social media*. Oxford University Press, 2018.

4

THE SOCIAL MEDIA ECOSYSTEM

Today's digital world provides many different social media platforms for communication. Each platform has its unique storytelling medium that enables their user base to share content snippets: Facebook is for longer posts and group posts, Instagram is for photo sharing, Snapchat is for ephemeral photos, TikTok is for short video sharing, to name a few. However, at the core, all social media platforms share the same fundamental concept: they are made up of users, who post content, and interact with other users and content.

This chapter describes a social media platform in terms of four elements: User, Content, Interaction and Algorithm. The interactions between these four elements are crucial in the mechanisms of information spread and provide the grounds for Bots to operate and accelerate the spread of influence.

Social Media Platforms

The **social media ecosystem** encapsulates the variety of social media platforms, the social media users, the content the users create, the user-user and user-content interactions, and the recommendation algorithm of the platform they reside in. The social media ecosystem can be broken down into social media platforms. A **social media platform** is an internet-based application for social networking and communication. Examples of modern day social media platforms are: Facebook, Reddit, X, TikTok and RedNote. For example, "Facebook" or "Facebook ecosystem" refers to the corresponding User-Content-Interactions-Algorithm system on the Facebook platform. A social media platform can further be broken down with language and geographical ecosystem. "English Facebook" refers to the Facebook content that are written in English". "United States Facebook" refers to the content from human users that originate from or affiliate with the United States, or content referring to events happening in the United States. **Figure 4.1** lays out the components of the social media ecosystem.

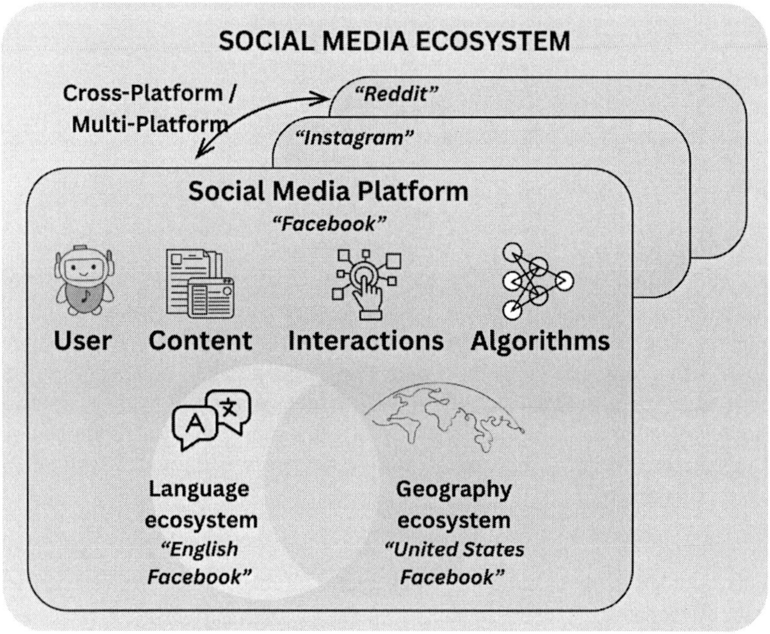

Figure 4.1: Components of the social media ecosystem

A **multi-platform** ecosystem occurs when different platforms fuse together because some elements are similar. Multi-platform studies examine the patterns of occurrence of the same elements across multiple social media platforms. Sometimes, these studies are called **cross-platforms**, when the elements are exactly the same. For example, multi-platform URLs refers to the study of sets of URLs that occur across two online ecosystems. A more detailed cross-platform study would study the occurrences where the URLs are exactly the same in the two ecosystems. The presence of the same URLs can provide clues to clusters of users that propagate the same thematic narratives across multiple platforms. Such narrative flow is common during major events like elections. For example, during the 2020 US elections, common sets of URLs linked the flow of narratives between Facebook, Reddit and X[102].

[102] Murdock, Isabel, Kathleen M. Carley, and Osman Yağan. "Identifying cross-platform user relationships in 2020 us election fraud and protest discussions." *Online Social Networks and Media* 33 (2023): 100245.

As we uncover how Bots behave on social media platforms, let us begin with an overview of the organization of these platforms. We cover some of the core platforms that make up much of the research for this book. There are platforms that we did not cover, and there will be platforms that have yet to come. As platforms evolve, the behavior of Bots will evolve to make full use of the functionalities. Current platform behavior may provide reference for future platform behavior and help us understand the evolution of platforms.

It is useful to characterize social media platforms using two dimensions: community organization and storytelling media. Community organization refers to the type of information presented and recommended to the user when the user first enters the platform's landing page, the first page the user sees. Storytelling media refers to the medium that the platform provides for users to create content. **Table 4.1** summarizes the structures of common social media platforms.

Community Organization. Social media platforms provide a virtual space to form communities. These communities form in one of two ways: by connections of social peers, or by the user's interests. The user's landing page is updated correspondingly. A peer-based platform means the user's landing page predominantly contains updates from his peers. An interest-based platform means the landing page is curated from the user's indicated or inferred interests.

Platform (feature)	**Community Organization** (Peer-Based/ Interest-Based)	**Storytelling Media** (Text/ Image/ Video/ Audio/ Interactive)
Facebook (posts)	Peer-Based	Text, Image
Facebook (stories)	Peer-Based	Image, Video
Instagram (posts, stories)	Peer-Based	Text, Image
Instagram (reels)	Peer-Based	Video
X	Peer-Based	Text, Image
RedNote	Peer-Based	Text, Image
Reddit	Interest-Based	Text, Image
TikTok	Interest-Based	Video
Clubhouse	Interest-Based	Audio
RecRoom, Roblox	Interest-Based	Interactive

Table 4.1: Summary of structures of social media platforms

A large number of social media platforms are peer-based, centered around user relationship interactions. These interactions typically form as such: a user follows other users, typically users he knows from real-life interactions, like his college mates or work colleagues. Social media companies have also invested in recommendation algorithms to expand a user's relationship base, by recommending other users that he might be interested in. These users can be friends of friends or other users who indicate similar traits (i.e., location). These platforms include: Facebook, Instagram and X.

In interest-based platforms, users indicate their interests and their feed is curated based on user-defined indications. Users indicate such interest by following topics and posts generated within topical threads. In Reddit, interest is indicated by joining a subreddit. In Roblox, interest is indicated by playing specific games. Recommendation systems on interest-based platforms identify the topics that users like based on a combination of implicit and explicit feedback. TikTok employs such a recommendation system to capture interest signals[103]. Implicit feedback is gathered from viewing behavior such as the amount of time spent on a post, and explicit feedback is gathered from interaction actions taken such as liking a post and following a content creator.

Storytelling Media. Every content post on a social media platform tells part of a story of a user's life, authentic or not. A variety of media can be used to tell stories: text, audio, video, and virtual interactions. A social media platform can be designed for users to tell their stories using one or more of these media, and the media offered by the platform can change over time.

Text-based social media platforms brought about the turn of social media ecosystem. They include Facebook and X (then Twitter). Such posts are primarily a string of text, and the platform is designed for the ease of reading and communication via texts, reflective from a huge central column designed for a text post.

Social media platforms then evolved to image-based platforms, where users primarily uploaded an image, or a series of images as a post. They include Instagram and SnapChat.. They also attach a caption to the post to describe the image and its context. This is a popular mode of storytelling on

---

[103] Wang, Pengda. "Recommendation algorithm in TikTok: Strengths, dilemmas, and possible directions." *Int'l J. Soc. Sci. Stud.* 10 (2022): 60.; Narayanan, Arvind. "Understanding Social Media Recommendation Algorithms." *Knight First Amendment Institute*, (2023).

Instagram. The platform designs its user pages around photo grids of user-posted photos.

From images come moving pictures, which make for video-based social media platforms. Videos are a combination of images and audio mediums. This is a popular medium for TikTok and Instagram (reels). These platforms organize their interface through full-screen videos and create an endless scrolling experience for users to watch video after video.

Specifically using the audio medium is a platform like Clubhouse. Clubhouse was released in August 2020. Users used the VOIP protocol to communicate with each other through Rooms. Its interface centers around icons representing Rooms and other users.

The new kid on the block is interactive media. This refers to social ecosystems in virtual reality space, such as Roblox and RecRoom. Users interact with each other within applications, games and virtual reality space. Such interactions also make use of tactile feedback through controllers. Some of these interactive platforms can be considered super-apps. They contain smaller applications and for unique and self-organizing user groups. For example, each Roblox game connects users through their interest in the particular game, and there are separate forums and chat threads for the discussion of tactics of each game.

Social Media Primitives

One could think of social media platforms as being made up of four elements: (1) users, (2) content, (3) interactions, and (4) the algorithm. These four are the social media primitives. The platform is a virtual venue that hosts people to connect with each other, and provide certain affordances to facilitate communication. The users generate and consume content through their online conversations, which manifests as posts, comments and other forms. In this space, users create new connections to interact with each other, like expressing a like on a post someone else made.

The fourth element, the algorithm, is controlled by the platform, which determines which content or user is recommended to others, and the affordances by which users can interact. Users can design their content to take advantage of these algorithms, which can in turn affect their interactions. One way of designing content that can attract more User-Content interactions from other users is to embed cognitive bias triggers within the content, a technique that will be elaborated in Chapter 7.

However, when social media platforms change their algorithms, the content that gets created and the users that posts can dramatically change. For example, when Twitter changed its algorithm to allow longer messages allowed for longer and more thoughtful content. When Facebook promoted certain news sites during election seasons, there were complaints over privacy concerns and news feed biases[104].

This User-Content-Interaction-Algorithm frame is useful to analyze how social media platforms encourage user participation, mediate content visibility, and shape the interaction dynamics between user and content. This frame allows a structured perspective to analyzing the patterns of online influence within social media platforms. For ease of writing, this frame might be abbreviated as **UCIA.**

User. The user is the one using the social media platform. This user can either be automated or manual: Bot or human. A user has an account, which is the user's persona. Users use accounts to participate in the online conversations, and consists of the identity the user discloses through his posts. In commonspeak, as well as in this book, the terms "user" and "account" are used interchangeably. An **actor** is an actively contributing user, whose actions affect the other users on social media platforms. Everyone is a user, but some users are actors, and others are lurkers that passively consume content. The **operator** refers to the human person who controls the social media account. For human accounts, the operator is usually the human himself. For Bot accounts, the operator is the human who controls and programs the Bot account. The operator can control one or more accounts.

Content. Social media platforms revolve around and are sustained by user-generated content. Content are articles and information created by users and posted on the platform and are dependent on the storytelling media available on the social media platforms. Generically, the manifestation of Content is called a **post.**

There are many ways to differentiate types of content. One common distinction is between original and repeated content. **Original content,**

---

[104] Hargreaves, Eduardo, Claudio Agosti, Daniel Menasché, Giovanni Neglia, Alexandre Reiffers-Masson, and Eitan Altman. "Biases in the facebook news feed: a case study on the italian elections." In *2018 IEEE/ACM International Conference on Advances in Social Networks Analysis and Mining (ASONAM)*, pp. 806-812. IEEE, 2018.

sometimes called **original posts**, is new and novel material authored by the user. This is in the form of a new post, an image or a commentary that contributes fresh perspectives to the online conversation. **Repeated Content**, on the other hand, involves re-circulating existing material. These contents are repeated in the form of retweets or shares of another user's posts. Quotes are a mixture between original and repeated content, where another user's post is quoted, but original thought is added to it.

Besides novelty and repetition, content can also be differentiated by stance. A **stance** is an opinion towards a target entity. The target entity can be an issue, a person or a product. The stance is usually represented as pro, neutral or anti. A pro stance indicates support, an anti stance indicates opposition or resistance, and a neutral stance does not indicate sides. A post can express one of these stances towards an entity or multiple entities.

Interactions. Social media platforms were conceptualized for people to interact virtually with other people. Interactions are the ways users communicate and engage with each other in the digital space. Interactions can either be user-content interactions or user-user interactions. User-content interactions are actions users perform on a Content item, such as tagging a user in a post, sharing a post, replying to a post etc. User-user interactions are performed on other users in the network, such as following or friending another user, which builds the peer-relationships of a user's network. Users can form interactions with many other users, who may form reciprocal interactions with the original users.

Algorithm. Algorithms are the hidden engines of the social media platform. The algorithm of the social media platform is a set of computational rules and machine learning systems that curate what content a user sees, how content is prioritized and ranked, and which interactions are made visible. In a sense, the algorithm governs the circulation of attention. However, the mechanics of these algorithms are usually proprietary and rarely transparent to the public, so users, researchers and analysts must often infer their workings from the patterns of visibility and engagement of their content[105].

While all social media platforms use machine learning models to maximize the user engagement on their platforms, the specific metrics that they prioritize – such as watch time, social connections, or recency – vary significantly. One way to make sense of these systems is to classify them

---

[105] Klinger, Ulrike, and Jakob Svensson. "The end of media logics? On algorithms and agency." *New media & society* 20, no. 12 (2018): 4653-4670.

by their discovery logic, or the principles by which these algorithms recommend and surface content to users to their user feed. The **user feed** is the primary interface through which people encounter content and other users on the platform. It is the screen that users first meet when they open the social media application. It is also called the **landing page** or **For You Page.** Broadly, algorithms fall into three categories: User-based discovery algorithm, Content-based discovery algorithm, and a hybrid discovery algorithm.

User-based discovery algorithms prioritize content based on the users' social ties. For example, Facebook's News Feed is anchored in the social graph, and surfaces posts from friends, family and groups to the user's feed[106]. LinkedIn operates similarly, emphasizing a user's professional network and feeds content that is popular among a user's first-degree connections.

In user-based discovery algorithms, the reach of the content depends heavily on the relationships the users built with each other and the influence of the users. User-User relationships are built through mechanisms like adding other users as friends, following other users, or connecting with other users. The influence of the user depends on metrics such as whether the user is a verified user on the platform, and the number of followers the user has. Verified users can be identified through icons like a badge on LinkedIn or a checkmark on X. These users have enhanced credibility and therefore visibility on the platform.

Content-based discovery algorithms focus on what is posted rather than social connections. TikTok exemplifies this approach. The TikTok For You Page rapidly learns from user behavior such as watch completion, replays, interactions with captions and audio, to promote content to the user. Often, these contents are from creators outside the set of accounts the user follows. Instagram Reels also employ a similar algorithm, feeding users videos that are already engaging a wide audience.

Hybrid discovery algorithm. Many platforms blend social and content signals. For example, X combines hashtags, trending topics and keywords with the user's social connections. The user feed displays posts not only from accounts that the user follows, but also from accounts outside their connections that are relevant. This relevance can be through topical

---

[106] Ugander, Johan, Brian Karrer, Lars Backstrom, and Cameron Marlow. "The anatomy of the facebook social graph." *arXiv preprint arXiv:1111.4503* (2011).

relevance or second-degree social ties (i.e., accounts followed by people the user already follows, posts liked by accounts the user already follows). Instagram's Feed ranks posts by recency and social connections, while its Reels system prioritizes watch time and broad engagement.

Social media platforms and primitives. Social media platforms have similar and unique ways of naming their primitives. Some platforms have multiple types of one primitive. For example, Instagram has three types of Content primitives: posts, reels and stories. **Table 4.2** summarizes the primitives across common platforms.

Platform	Primitive	Terminology
Facebook	User	User
	Content	Posts, Stories
	Interactions	Add as Friend, Share a Post, Comment on Post
	Algorithm	Hybrid
X	User	User
	Content	Tweet
	Interactions	Following a user, Tagging a user, Retweet, Quote, Reply
	Algorithm	Hybrid
Instagram	User	User
	Content	Posts, Reels, Stories
	Interactions	Following a User, Share a Post, Comment on Post
	Algorithm	User-based (Feed), Content-based (Reels)
Reddit	User	User
	Content	Post
	Interactions	Following a user, Following a subreddit, Comment on Post
	Algorithm	User-based
TikTok	User	User
	Content	TikToks
	Interactions	Following a User, Share a Post, Comment on Post
	Algorithm	Content-based
RedNote	User	User
	Content	Notes
	Interactions	Following a User, Share a Post, Comment on Post
	Algorithm	Content based

Table 4.2: Mapping of Social Media Primitives for core platforms

In analyzing social media, it is not feasible to analyze all the users or all the content, or all the interactions. Therefore, we have to set boundaries in the analysis. In setting boundaries, we usually intentionally pick interesting contexts to study and represent specific parts of the social network. Common ways of setting boundaries are topically using keywords, or geographically using bounding boxes, or by language. For example, to find posts that relate to the pop star Taylor Swift concert, we might search the posts by the hashtag #taylorswiftconcert, or collect posts geolocated within the cities that she is performing in, or run a passive background stream to collect tweets related to the hashtag as they are posted live. The options for boundary settings depends on the platform's algorithms and the cost structure for data collection, and not on what the analyst wants to do.

Following the boundary setting, we typically form a network graph. In such network graphs, the nodes represent users or content, and edges or links represent interactions. For example, if the nodes are users in X, the edges could represent all the interaction mechanics available, such as following, retweeting, mentioning, liking and so on. If the nodes are URLs or hashtags, the edges could represent co-occurrence of these artifacts in the message. Sometimes, nodes are colored in different colors to represent different types of users, like using a red color for Bots and green for humans.

Another type of analysis is an ego-centered network analysis, which typically focuses on a single user. This focal individual is called the **ego user**, or ego for short. **Neighbors** are users directly connected with the ego through interactions, representing the ego's immediate social circle. All other users in the network are called **alters.** Analysts then apply social network analysis methods and AI to analyze these networks.

Figure 4.2 illustrates a simple network graph formed during the analysis of social networks. The network graph would be used as the primary visualization format throughout this book.

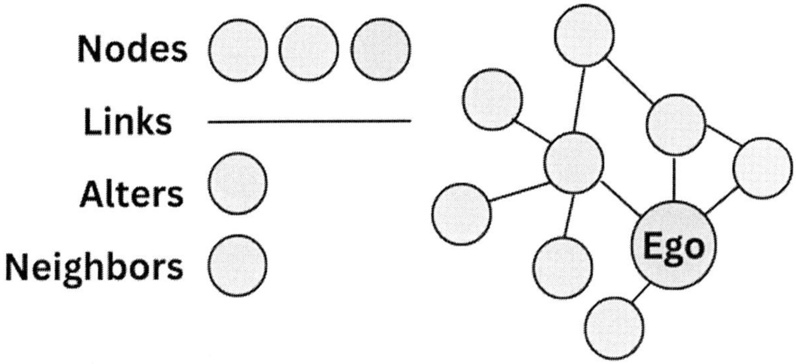

Figure 4.2: Illustration of a simple network graph that is formed during analysis of social networks

This set of social media primitives enable social media mechanics. **Social media mechanics** are actions that a single user can perform on a social media account. Social media mechanics enable users to perform four main functions: content generation, content reactions, content dissemination, and network building/ dissolutions. Content generation involves creating and commenting on posts, the act of putting one's thoughts and stories online for other users to view and interact with. Content reactions involve liking or disliking a post, and adding reactions to a post. Reactions are an expression of approval or disapproval towards a post. Content dissemination mechanics involve sharing a post both within and cross-platforms, and tagging another user. Typically, users share posts of topics that are interesting and valuable to themselves or to broadcast a message[107]. Users tag other users in a post to bring the content to the tagged users attention and bring the tagged users into the conversation. Finally, network building/ dissolution mechanics involve actions that change who is talking to whom, and who is reading whose posts. One such action is following another user, or unfollowing another user. Another is mentioning a user so that they get recommended by the platform to users to follow them. Another such action is reposting someone's message which causes more users to see it and so potentially read it. Such mechanics build relationship interactions.

---

[107] Cosme, Danielle, Christin Scholz, Hang-Yee Chan, Bruce P. Doré, Prateekshit Pandey, José Carreras-Tartak, Nicole Cooper, Alexandra Paul, Shannon M. Burns, and Emily B. Falk. "Message self and social relevance increases intentions to share content: Correlational and causal evidence from six studies." *Journal of Experimental Psychology: General* 152, no. 1 (2023): 253.

The variety of social media mechanics that a user can perform depends on thc affordances of the platforms. For example, Reddit has the downvote function to express a dislike reaction to a content, but this function is not available on Facebook. Each platform has its own nomenclature for similar mechanics. For example, the function that allows for sharing a post is named as “retweet” on X and “share” on Facebook. This naming differences reflect how the algorithms are designed differently to prioritize and differentiate social media mechanics, and shape the interpretation and social meaning of the mechanic. For example, “retweet” on X indicates amplification, whereas “share” on Instagram indicates casual sharing. Such branding reflects how users engage with the mechanic and thus drives patterns of engagement[108].

One common network graph used to represent the social interactions is the **Agent x Agent -- All Communication Network**. In such a notation, “Agent x Agent” means that the node types Agent and Agent are linked together by the link “All Communication”. All Communication refers to all communication mechanics on the platform. For example, if the graph represents the platform X, All Communication would be retweets, @mentions, quotes and replies. An Agent x Agent – All Communication Network graph would mean that the nodes represent agents, and two agents are linked together if there were any form of communication as afforded by the platform between them.

Social Media Actors

A social media actor is a user that actively contributes content to a social media platform, and the actor’s actions affect other users. The content does not have to be original; the social media user just needs to be posting content. The social media actor can create content or form relationships, which can change both the narrative and the network structure in social media space.

There are many types of actors. They may be humans, Bots, cyborgs (human-in-the-loop automation), or organizations. They may be private actors or state-sponsored actors. Whether an actor is an individual or an organization or a state-sponsored actor, they can control one or many accounts (including automated ones), pursue different purposes across those

---

[108] DeVito, Michael Ann, Jeremy Birnholtz, and Jeffery T. Hancock. "Platforms, people, and perception: Using affordances to understand self-presentation on social media." In *Proceedings of the 2017 ACM conference on computer supported cooperative work and social computing*, pp. 740-754. 2017.

accounts, and run different scales of operations. **Figure 4.3** sketches a typical view of such scale: individuals typically manage a handful of accounts, organizations run dozens to hundreds of accounts, and state operations can coordinate thousands of accounts because they have larger human and equipment resources.

Individuals are typically single, independent users that have their own agenda. These agenda include posting trivia about their personal life or updates on professional achievements or expressing political views. Some hold official and personal identities that serve different mandates. For example, the X account *realDonaldTrump* is a personal handle for the person Donald Trump, and *POTUS* is an institutional handle for the office of the president. Both accounts represent the same person but can speak with distinct voices and objectives. Individuals also commonly compartmentalize activity across multiple handles. For example, I have an Instagram handle that is a private one for personal updates, and a handle *littlebabypenguin* that is public for work and travel related news. In each of these cases, the individuals may or may not automate the account with Bots. But if automation is used, it is usually small-scale and lightly used.

Individuals who cultivate large followings function as “influencers”. Their posts are immediately delivered to a huge number of audiences and are more likely to be engaged with, therefore more likely to be amplified by the platform’s algorithms. Any message that they share have the potential to propagate widely. In network science terms, they often sit at high centrality positions, therefore they can shape the agenda and mobilize action within their communities with relatively little effort. An example of an influencer is Taylor Swift. Her Instagram account *taylorsiwft* has 282 million followers. A single post that she made can achieve 2.7 million likes and 536,000 shares within 2 days, which speaks to how vast her message can spread.

Individuals can and do create Bots. *PepitoTheCat* is a Bot on X platform that was created by Clement Storck in 2011 in France[109]. Typically, individuals only create a small number of Bots and occasionally purchase Bots to boost engagement of their posts. Such Bot activity is usually visible but is isolated to the individual and not coordinated across large networks. The use of Cyborgs are common within individuals: a person writes or

[109] https://en.wikipedia.org/wiki/PepitoTheCat

curates content while scripts from third-party tools like X Pro[110] handle timing, templating and cross-posting[111].

Organizations. An organizational account is owned by a private or public entity and speaks with the institution's voice. Such entities include: a company, a news room, a non-profit organization, a university, an agency, to name a few. A post on the account is treated as an official statement of the organization, not the personal views of the staffer who wrote the message. Organizational accounts may have multiple people (i.e., communications team, public relations team, social media managers, editors) that share access to the account to create content and craft statements. With a team behind the account, it is possible for organizational accounts to publish on an editorial calendar, have more consistent styles, and sustain a higher posting frequency than a single individual.

More broadly, organizations lean on automation for (i) distribution of messages through automatic posting of headlines to social channels. For example, the *nytimes* is the X handle of the news agency New York Times, which uses Bots to announce news stories automatically[112]. Organizations also use Bots for (ii) alerts and customer care, to triage frequently asked questions, or provide status updates. For example, the non-profit organizations Invisible People use Bots to deliver basic information to homeless people in need and connect them with services[113]. A small team of people enable these organizations to provide systematic and repeatable communications to the public. Finally, organizations can use Bots for structured updates like templated posts for the weather, sports or event reminders. *weatherchannel* is the X handle of The Weather Channel, a weather broadcasting organization based on Atlanta, United States. It posts weather forecasts updates and weather disasters.

State-sponsored actors are social media accounts that are operated by, or funded by, or closely aligned with a government. Their communications

---

[110] https://pro.x.com/

[111] Ng, Lynnette Hui Xian, Dawn C. Robertson, and Kathleen M. Carley. "Cyborgs for strategic communication on social media." *Big Data & Society* 11, no. 1 (2024): 20539517241231275.

[112] https://gijn.org/stories/journalism-bots-a-quick-history-and-ideas-for-use-in-your-newsroom/

[113] Kanter, Beth, and Allison Fine. "Leveraging the Power of Bots for Civil Society." *Stanford Social Innovation Review*, April 11, 2018. https://doi.org/10.48558/YJPC-K672

typically advance the military, economic or political interests and objectives of a state. Their messages can be treated as institutional speech. The post speaks for the state, or a state organ, or a government. Posts have typically gotten official approval from a higher power in the country, and do not represent the personal views of the individual staffer that typed it. Many such accounts use a mix of official outlets and covert assets. One type of state-sponsored actors are overt state media are RT (X handle *RT_com*) and Sputnik International (X handle *SputnikInt*), which are closely linked to the Russian government. Another type are the covert state-aligned actors that coordinate across many accounts and platforms to spread state-directed narratives[114].

State-sponsored actors frequently rely on automation and coordinated account fleets from Bots to scale narrative distribution. Empirical studies show that Russian Bots on X show substantial automated participation in contentious political periods[115], and campaign-level analyses of the Russian-Ukraine conflict document Bot-driven pro-Kremlin narratives and counter-messaging dynamics across different phases of the war[116]. China exemplifies the use of both overt and covert tactics. There are large-scale state-organized posts that flood social media discourse with positive and patriotic messages manufacture support[117]. The Chinese government also coordinate Bots to seed and amplify preferred frames, especially during crises and foreign-policy events[118].

---

114 https://demtech.oii.ox.ac.uk/wp-content/uploads/sites/12/2021/01/CyberTroop-Report-2020-v.2.pdf

115 Stukal, Denis, Sergey Sanovich, Richard Bonneau, and Joshua A. Tucker. "Detecting bots on Russian political Twitter." *Big data* 5, no. 4 (2017): 310-324. ; Casas Mas, Belén. "Mapping the Terrain of Digital Warfare: A Bibliometric Analysis of Russian Propaganda During Armed Conflicts." (2025).

116 Fredheim, Rolf. *Virtual Manipulation Brief-Verified Propagandists and the Hamas-Israel War*. NATO Strategic Communications Centre of Excellence, 2023.

117 Ji, Jiaojiao, Ting Hu, Zihang Chen, and Mengxiao Zhu. "Exploring the climate change discourse on Chinese social media and the role of social bots." *Asian Journal of Communication* 34, no. 1 (2024): 109-128. ; Lu, Yingdan, and Jennifer Pan. "Capturing clicks: How the Chinese government uses clickbait to compete for visibility." *Political Communication* 38, no. 1-2 (2021): 23-54.

118 Bolsover, Gillian, and Philip Howard. "Chinese computational propaganda: Automation, algorithms and the manipulation of information about Chinese politics on Twitter and Weibo." *Information, communication & society* 22, no. 14 (2019): 2063-2080.; Thunø, Mette, and Kristoffer Laigaard Nielbo. "The initial digitalization of

Positive use of Bots by state-sponsored actors spread pro-government messages and messages for social good. During the coronavirus pandemic of 2020, governments used Bots to promote community-focused actions like social distancing to limit the transmission of the virus, and public motivation during the dreary pandemic[119]. State-sponsored actors can also use Bots for malicious influence and information operations campaign, especially to influence the psychological leaning of users from other states. The Kremlin extensively uses Bots for information manipulation attempts towards Ukraine by producing targeted anti-Ukraine and pro-Russian posts on X[120]. Similarly, China hosts the 50-cent army, where government-sponsored social media actors were paid 50 cents for each time they posted messages online [121]. This army typically posts emotive messages about government or political issues to direct citizen rage away from the authorities.

Summary. Different types of actors are more influential on different social media platforms, hence it is important to understand the characteristics of the types of actors and their behavior. Actors may have accounts on multiple platforms and may post different sets of narratives or styles on different platforms. For example Taylor Swift's Instagram page promotes her upcoming albums using pictures of herself and album art, making use of the visual photo grid of the Instagram platform. On the more text-based platform X, she puts headlines "And, baby, that's show business for you. New album The Life of a Showgirl. Out October 3". Further, Bots on different platforms tend to have different styles. For example, Facebook Bots tend to be more conversational in nature, while X Bots are more

---

Chinese diplomacy (2019–2021): establishing global communication networks on Twitter." *Journal of Contemporary China* 33, no. 146 (2024): 244-266.

[119] Sutton, Jeannette, Scott L. Renshaw, and Carter T. Butts. "The first 60 days: American public health agencies' social media strategies in the emerging COVID-19 pandemic." *Health security* 18, no. 6 (2020): 454-460.

[120] Marigliano, Rebecca, Lynnette Hui Xian Ng, and Kathleen M. Carley. "Analyzing digital propaganda and conflict rhetoric: a study on Russia's bot-driven campaigns and counter-narratives during the Ukraine crisis." *Social Network Analysis and Mining* 14, no. 1 (2024): 170. ; Smart, Bridget, Joshua Watt, Sara Benedetti, Lewis Mitchell, and Matthew Roughan. "# IStandWithPutin versus# IStandWithUkraine: the interaction of bots and humans in discussion of the Russia/Ukraine war." In *International Conference on Social Informatics*, pp. 34-53. Cham: Springer International Publishing, 2022.

[121] Bolsover, Gillian. "Social media, computational propaganda, and control in China and beyond." In *The World Information War*, pp. 122-138. Routledge, 2021.

political in nature[122]. Influential accounts in Weibo that post about the US-China Trade War in 2019 tend to be media and commentator accounts, while those in X are predominantly politicians, media and organizations[123]. Recognizing these dynamics is essential, as actors deploy Bots differently and strategically to achieve their agendas, depending on the affordances and audience demographics of the platform.

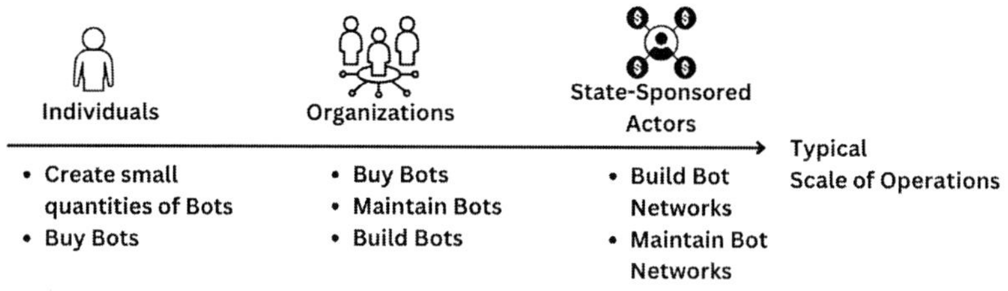

Figure 4.3: Typical Scale of Bot Operations and Usage of the social media actors

---

[122] Obadimu, Adewale, Esther Mead, Samer Al-Khateeb, and Nitin Agarwal. "A comparative analysis of Facebook and Twitter bots." (2019).

[123] Yang, Yi, Jia-Huey Hsu, Karl Löfgren, and Wonhyuk Cho. "Cross-platform comparison of framed topics in Twitter and Weibo: machine learning approaches to social media text mining." *Social Network Analysis and Mining* 11, no. 1 (2021): 75.

5

Bots vs Humans

Bot and human accounts exhibit systematic differences in how they affiliate themselves, communicate, and interact online. Many studies focus on posting frequency, noting that Bots often produce almost twice as many posts as humans[124] and can be active during nocturnal hours[125]. However, posting volume is only one marker. Bots and humans diverge systematically across other dimensions of online behavior. This chapter explores the differences between the two species across four dimensions: linguistic signatures, social affiliations, network topologies, and topic profiles. Understanding these patterns pave the way for reliable identification of bot accounts, which also provides a foundation for examining automated influence campaigns.

Understanding these contrasts clarifies the capabilities and limits of Bots versus humans. Bots are good at providing scale, speed and consistency, while humans are good at creating nuances in replies and maintaining personal relationships. With such knowledge, humans and Bots can work together more productively and distribute the workload.

Linguistic Signatures

Linguistic signatures are patterns of how an account uses language. The linguistic signature is typically a measurable profile that persists across a

---

[124] Stieglitz, Stefan, Florian Brachten, Davina Berthelé, Mira Schlaus, Chrissoula Venetopoulou, and Daniel Veutgen. "Do social bots (still) act different to humans?– Comparing metrics of social bots with those of humans." In *International conference on social computing and social media*, pp. 379-395. Cham: Springer International Publishing, 2017. ; Gilani, Zafar, Reza Farahbakhsh, Gareth Tyson, and Jon Crowcroft. "A large-scale behavioural analysis of bots and humans on twitter." *ACM Transactions on the Web (TWEB)* 13, no. 1 (2019): 1-23.

[125] Grinberg, Nir, Mor Naaman, Blake Shaw, and Gilad Lotan. "Extracting diurnal patterns of real world activity from social media." In *Proceedings of the International AAAI Conference on Web and Social Media*, vol. 7, no. 1, pp. 205-214. 2013.

user's posts and distinguishes one actor (or one actor type) from another. Computationally, the linguistic signature of an actor is measured as a feature vector computed on single posts then aggregated over a window.

One method used to identify linguistic signatures is to extract **psycholinguistic cues**, which are features in sentences that facilitate word recognition and meaning construction. Such cues include semantic cues (e.g., number of first-person pronouns used, number of second-person pronouns used, Flesch-Kincaid reading difficulty of the text etc.), emotion cues (e.g., number of abusive terms used, number of negative terms used etc), and metadata cues (number of URLs or hashtags used etc). These cues can be extracted using software like NetMapper[126].

Bots and humans have different linguistic signatures, or writing styles. Bots are often pre-programmed with defined sentence structures, making their output more rigid, while humans are more fluid in their writing, reflecting their spontaneity and contextual thought. The most obvious programmed style is the use of templates. A classic example is a Bot that is spreading news, which delivers updates in fixed formats, such as "BREAKING NEWS: <date> <time> <headline> <URL>". Such Bots have been found in Indonesian religious discourse on X[127].

Linguistic features provide fine-grained markers that differentiate automated Bot writing from human writing. Bots often use simpler and less diverse vocabulary than humans, often focusing on proper nouns while humans use more nuanced verb phrases and figurative language[128]. Bot messages also contain more URLs and hashtags, while human-authored posts contain greater syntactic variety and use more personal pronouns[129].

---

[126] https://netanomics.com/netmapper/

[127] Danaditya, Adya, Lynnette Hui Xian Ng, and Kathleen M. Carley. "From curious hashtags to polarized effect: profiling coordinated actions in indonesian twitter discourse." *Social Network Analysis and Mining* 12, no. 1 (2022): 105.

[128] Varol, Onur, Emilio Ferrara, Clayton Davis, Filippo Menczer, and Alessandro Flammini. "Online human-bot interactions: Detection, estimation, and characterization." In *Proceedings of the international AAAI conference on web and social media*, vol. 11, no. 1, pp. 280-289. 2017. ; Uyheng, Joshua, Lynnette Hui Xian Ng, and Kathleen M. Carley. "Active, aggressive, but to little avail: characterizing bot activity during the 2020 Singaporean elections." *Computational and Mathematical Organization Theory* 27, no. 3 (2021): 324-342.

[129] Cardaioli, Matteo, Mauro Conti, Andrea Di Sorbo, Enrico Fabrizio, Sonia Laudanna, and Corrado A. Visaggio. "It'sa matter of style: Detecting social bots

Content written by humans are more lexically diverse than Bot content, and organizational accounts, politicians and celebrities have the most lexically diverse content[130]. Even the use of LLMs does not necessarily create more human-like posts. Research experiments by Alafnan et. al., 2023 show that the GPT 4 models still have a lower lexical diversity and lower reading difficulty[131].

Another linguistic feature is the emotional tone. Bot content is overall less emotionally varied, and uses fewer markers of irony, humor and sarcasm. Bots use more abusive terms and expletives than humans[132], which lends them the power needed to spread hate speech. Bots are observed to be active participants in spreading hate speech and divisive messages. For example, during the 2020 coronavirus pandemic, Bot activity was linked to elevated levels of racially and nationality targeted hate speech[133]. Human users, on the other hand, naturally embed emotional nuances and their posts have higher variability in positive and negative affect terms[134], and are more heterogeneous across contexts and communities. The latest GPT model also

through writing style consistency." In *2021 international conference on computer communications and networks (ICCCN)*, pp. 1-9. IEEE, 2021.

[130] Inuwa-Dutse, Isa, Bello Shehu Bello, and Ioannis Korkontzelos. "Lexical analysis of automated accounts on Twitter." *arXiv preprint arXiv:1812.07947* (2018).

[131] AlAfnan, Mohammad Awad, and Siti Fatimah MohdZuki. "Do artificial intelligence chatbots have a writing style? An investigation into the stylistic features of ChatGPT-4." *Journal of Artificial intelligence and technology* 3, no. 3 (2023): 85-94. ; Ng, Lynnette Hui Xian, and Kathleen M. Carley. "Are LLM-Powered Social Media Bots Realistic?." *arXiv preprint arXiv:2508.00998* (2025).

[132] Stella, Massimo, Emilio Ferrara, and Manlio De Domenico. "Bots increase exposure to negative and inflammatory content in online social systems." *Proceedings of the National Academy of Sciences* 115, no. 49 (2018): 12435-12440. ; Ng, Lynnette Hui Xian, and Kathleen M. Carley. "A global comparison of social media bot and human characteristics." *Scientific Reports* 15, no. 1 (2025): 10973.

[133] Uyheng, Joshua, and Kathleen M. Carley. "Bots and online hate during the COVID-19 pandemic: case studies in the United States and the Philippines." *Journal of computational social science* 3, no. 2 (2020): 445-468.

[134] Chmiel, Anna, Julian Sienkiewicz, Mike Thelwall, Georgios Paltoglou, Kevan Buckley, Arvid Kappas, and Janusz A. Hołyst. "Collective emotions online and their influence on community life." *PloS one* 6, no. 7 (2011): e22207.

reflects the formulaic Bot language, often producing posts that begin with "It is disheartening"[135].

These linguistic signatures are useful not only for detecting Bots but also for interpreting their strategies. Bots' reliance on amplification cues and emotionally restrained content reflect their primary function as information broadcasters and disseminators in an influence campaign, whereas human language reflects organic social engagement.

Summary. Linguistic signatures are persistent patterns of language use that differentiate actors online. These signatures can be measured through psycholinguistic, semantic and emotional cues. Features such as pronoun use, reading difficulty, lexical diversity or the prevalence of URLs and hashtags reveal systematic differences in how accounts communicate. Humans generally display spontaneity and stylistic variation while Bots tend towards rigid templated sentence structures. While humans convey richer, more affective variety and embed subtle emotional cues, Bots use narrower sets of vocabularies and often rely on abusive or polarizing language. Even advanced LLM-generated outputs retain a formulaic style that echoes traditional Bot signatures. These linguistic signatures reflect how Bots lean on simplified, restrained language to broadcast and spread content rapidly, while human language reflects the complexity of organic engagement and community exchange.

Social Affiliations

A social affiliation is the set of groups, roles and places that an account publicly aligns with. Examples of affiliations are: political parties, professional occupations, religious communities or locations. In the digital environment, social affiliations are inferred from the information that a user makes publicly available. This information can come from the profile metadata (e.g., labels on the user bio, declared location, text that is part of the user handle), content signals (e.g., hashtags used), and interactions (e.g., who the account follows, mentions, replies to etc). On social media platforms, individuals can deliberately highlight or even mask their social affiliations. Looking at social affiliations are important because these affiliations shape not only how individuals present themselves, but also

---

[135] Ng, Lynnette Hui Xian, Bianca NY Kang, and Kathleen M. Carley. "AuraSight: Generating Realistic Social Media Data." *Carnegie Mellon University Technical Reports* (2025).

how they interact, form communities and organize collective action[136]. Such activity influences patterns of information sharing and social influence online, and can reinforce echo chambers, enable coordinated mobilization, or be strategically manipulated for influence.

Affiliation and identity are related but not the same. An identity is who the user claims to be and it carries a psychological meaning. Examples of identities are teacher, professor, mom, American etc. An affiliation is the formal connection to a group, for example, "faculty at Carnegie Mellon University", "based in Singapore". In practice, identity is a person's overall sense of self, while social affiliation is relationships that an individual have to other things, persons and locations[137]. While it is usually the identity that shapes how a person presents himself online, sometimes the online persona adopts an identity based on his affiliation.

Let us refer to a canonical stylized actor from the AuraSight scenario. The actor *jstan4ella* writes in his profile bio that he is an "EthalianFan" and his location is from "Ethal". "Ella" is the name of an Ethalian singer that represented the country in the songwriting competition. Given that the actor writes "4ella" in his user name and indicates that he is an Ethalian fan in his profile bio, we can infer that he affiliates himself with the fan base of Ella, an Ethalian singer. He takes on the identity of an Ethalian because he indicates that his location is from Ethal, and he is an Ethalian fan.

To understand how social affiliations and the associated identities shape behavior, we draw on Social Identity Theory. Social Identity Theory explains how actors associate themselves with roles and group memberships. To describe the results and variations in social affiliations and identity theory, we apply Social Cyber Geography as a method, which situates community interactions. Collectively, Social Identity Theory and the Social Cyber Geography helps us understand how actors anchor themselves socially and spatially in the social media ecosystem.

---

[136] Taylor, Sean J., Lev Muchnik, Madhav Kumar, and Sinan Aral. "Identity effects in social media." *Nature Human Behaviour* 7, no. 1 (2023): 27-37. ; Pan, Zhao, Yaobin Lu, Bin Wang, and Patrick YK Chau. "Who do you think you are? Common and differential effects of social self-identity on social media usage." *Journal of Management Information Systems* 34, no. 1 (2017): 71-101.

[137] Tajfel, Henri, and John C. Turner. "The social identity theory of intergroup behavior." In *Political psychology*, pp. 276-293. Psychology Press, 2004. ; Freeman, Linton C. "Filling in the blanks: A theory of cognitive categories and the structure of social affiliation." *Social Psychology Quarterly* (1992): 118-127.

Social identity theory argues that people describe themselves and others in terms of groups, i.e., identities. These identities come from all walks of life: occupation roles, like a teacher, or an engineer; family roles like mom, dad; religious roles like Christian or Buddhist; political roles like Republican or Democrat; or nationalities like American or British. Users make these identities visible through self-presentation. They disclose or signal aspects of their identity in their user bio, user names or post content to align with particular communities. In a user's social media profile, they can describe themselves using identity terms. For example, they can write in their profile bio or description, "Ethalian", or put an Ethalian flag to signal that they identify with being an Ethalian. In their social media posts, they can describe themselves or others using identity terms. For example, they can write "I am a mom too", or "As a teacher,..". These identity terms (e.g., "teacher", "mom") are known as identity cues.

Bots strategically exploit identity cues to mimic legitimacy and blend in with target audiences. They often adopt common combinations of identities, such as those tied to gender and political stereotypes, to align with human expectations and appear more credible[138]. For example, Bots that spread financial (dis)information include in their user profile many finance identities like "investors", "bitcoins" and so forth. Further, Bots frequently align their content with the identities they present[139]. That is, Bots identifying with political identities tend to engage more in political discourse, while those with family-related identities discuss more home-owner and familial themes.

Bots also interact with other users who include similar identities in their profile. For example, they retweet users that are of similar political affiliations or nationalities[140]. In 2016, the United Kingdom European Union (UK EU) held a referendum vote to decide whether the UK should remain a member of the EU. This referendum, known as the Brexit referendum, had two sides, the pro-Leave and pro-Remain camp. There were Bots on both sides that were promoting the corresponding campaign.

---

138 Phillips, Samantha C., Lynnette Hui Xian Ng, and Kathleen M. Carley. "Blended Bots: Infiltration through Identity Deception on Social Media." *arXiv preprint arXiv:2406.05246* (2024).

139 Ng, Lynnette Hui Xian, and Kathleen M. Carley. "A global comparison of social media bot and human characteristics." *Scientific Reports* 15, no. 1 (2025): 10973.

140 Ng, Lynnette Hui Xian, and Iain J. Cruickshank. "Recruitment promotion via twitter: a network-centric approach of analyzing community engagement using social identity." *Digital Government: Research and Practice* 4, no. 4 (2023): 1-17.

Regardless of the community the Bots affiliated themselves to through their user profile (i.e., “LeaveEUOfficial”), they had a clear focus on retweeting and amplifying the users of the same camp, as compared to users of the opposite camp, or users that did not display any affiliation[141].

Figure 5.1 illustrates the homophilic interactions of users with an all-communication network graph from the AuraSight scenario. The nodes are users, and these users are colored by the nationality listed in their profile. The links between nodes represent that the two users had a communication interaction. The clustering was performed using a force-atlas clustering algorithm[142]. This graph shows how people of the same nationality mainly interact with others of the same nationality, and that people of the same nationality are responding to each other in the same way. This illustrates how one’s identity (i.e., nationality) affects how they communicate: either by interacting with others of the same identity, or behaving similarly with the others of the same identity.

Identity signaling means putting an identity in either the content or the user profile. The systematic identity-content-interaction alignment of Bots underscores how they are programmed for predictability, and how they leverage identity signaling to influence desired communities.

---

[141] Bruno, Matteo, Renaud Lambiotte, and Fabio Saracco. "Brexit and bots: characterizing the behaviour of automated accounts on Twitter during the UK election." *EPJ Data Science* 11, no. 1 (2022): 17.

[142] Jacomy, Mathieu, Tommaso Venturini, Sebastien Heymann, and Mathieu Bastian. "ForceAtlas2, a continuous graph layout algorithm for handy network visualization designed for the Gephi software." *PloS one* 9, no. 6 (2014): e98679.

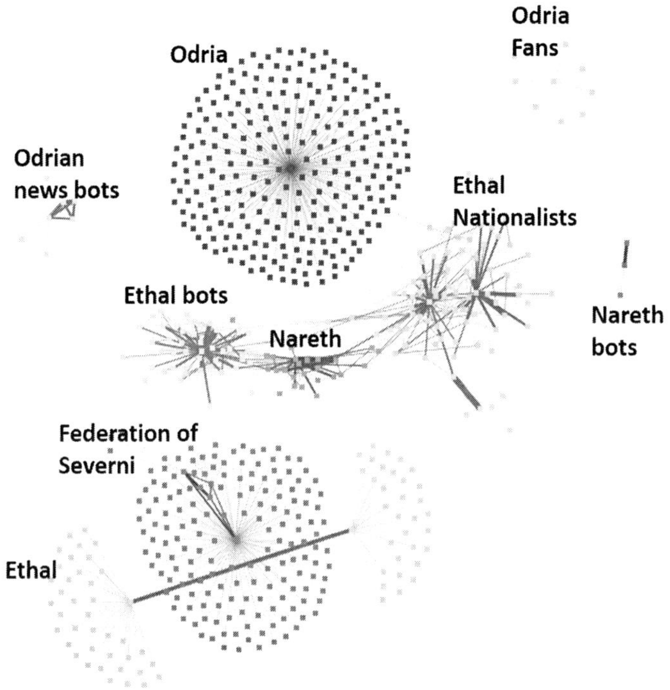

Figure 5.1: The All-Communication network graph of the first day of the AuraSight scenario. The nodes are users, and these users are colored by their nationality. Links between nodes represent that the two users had a communication interaction. The clustering shows how users tend to communicate with others of similar nationality.

A second expression of social affiliations is through locations. Locations can be shown on a user profile as an identity, either by listing "From United States" or the nationality "American". Most social media platforms have a location field which users can specifically list their location. Another way to identify a user's location is through subtle cues like the location of the text, or what time of day they are posting, or the slang and language used. Many social media platforms allow location-tagging to posts, and some like Instagram and SnapChat provide a map interface where posts tagged to a location would pop up in a small balloon. Further, base topics of a user's posting can provide indications of the user's location. For example, in discussion of a basketball game, users that typically talk about "celtics victory" are likely to come from Boston, while users that refer to "ohio bucks" are likely to originate from Lake Erie[143]. Here, we are going to focus on what users put in their user profile.

We can make sense of people's social affiliation towards location using the methodology of Social Cyber Geography (SCG). Social Cyber Geography conceptualizes the online space as an interconnected one with the physical world, where digital communities both mirror and reshape geographical patterns of interactions. This perspective treats online networks in harmony with the physical world: social interactions are not shaped only by shared topical interests or shared identities, but also by the common physical locations from which actors participate. Location-based social networks make visible how perceived proximity digital ties[144], such as user-to-user trust[145], mobility patterns[146] and community cohesion[147].

Bots, too, occupy this social cyber geography. Bot technology is pervasive. Anyone in the world can set up a Bot. Every country in the world has people or companies who have employed Bots. A Bot does not necessarily need to be affiliated with the country of its operator, although it should. A Bot can be affiliated with a country because the people who set that Bot up tag it with some kind of location information. As programmed accounts, Bots are not confined to specific regions, but are deployed worldwide. In several

---

[143] Eisenstein, Jacob, Brendan O'Connor, Noah A. Smith, and Eric Xing. "A latent variable model for geographic lexical variation." In *Proceedings of the 2010 conference on empirical methods in natural language processing*, pp. 1277-1287. 2010.

[144] Papangelis, Konstantinos, Alan Chamberlain, Ioanna Lykourentzou, Vassilis-Javed Khan, Michael Saker, Hai-Ning Liang, Irwyn Sadien, and Ting Cao. "Performing the digital self: Understanding location-based social networking, territory, space, and identity in the city." *ACM Transactions on Computer-Human Interaction (TOCHI)* 27, no. 1 (2020): 1-26.

[145] Fusco, Sarah Jean, Roba Abbas, Katina Michael, and Anas Aloudat. "Location-based social networking: impact on trust in relationships." *IEEE Technology and Society Magazine* 31, no. 2 (2012): 39-50.

[146] Cho, Eunjoon, Seth A. Myers, and Jure Leskovec. "Friendship and mobility: user movement in location-based social networks." In *Proceedings of the 17th ACM SIGKDD international conference on Knowledge discovery and data mining*, pp. 1082-1090. 2011.

[147] Valverde-Rebaza, Jorge C., Mathieu Roche, Pascal Poncelet, and Alneu de Andrade Lopes. "The role of location and social strength for friendship prediction in location-based social networks." *Information Processing & Management* 54, no. 4 (2018): 475-489.

studies that profile Bots throughout the globe, Bots are found to be affiliated with almost every country on the globe[148].

In fact, Bots are present in each country in 20% of the users that are also affiliated to that country based on the location name that is tagged in their user profile. This proportion is similar throughout all the countries. **Figure 5.2** shows the Bot distribution across the world during a study of twelve weeks of the 2020 coronavirus tweets from the platform X. Other studies of Bot affiliations during the coronavirus pandemic from millions of tweets also show an even distribution of Bots across the globe[149]. Note that in terms of location tagging, only 62% of the users can be tagged with locations. The other 38% of users either do not reveal their locations, or affiliate with generic or fictional locations like "earth", "space", "my bedroom".

Bots have specific location affiliations, which makes them strategically positioned to exploit geopolitical contexts for influence, specifically to amplify certain narratives in one region while suppressing others elsewhere. For example, if I am an operator of two Bots, one affiliated with Country A and another affiliated in Country B, I can use the first Bot to amplify narratives favorable to of Country A and the second Bot to depress narratives related to Country B. With such narrative manipulation, narratives related to Country A will be amplified more by social media algorithms, and more visible than narratives related to Country B.

Such strategic affiliation of Bots have been used for digital diplomacy, where Bots work in tandem with state and political actors to project a narrative favorable to the country[150]. During the 2023 US-China spat over an allegedly China-deployed balloon, Bots affiliated with the US were

---

148 Tan, Zhaoxuan, Shangbin Feng, Melanie Sclar, Herun Wan, Minnan Luo, Yejin Choi, and Yulia Tsvetkov. "BotPercent: Estimating Bot Populations in Twitter Communities." In *Findings of the Association for Computational Linguistics: EMNLP 2023*, pp. 14295-14312. 2023.; Qazi, Umair, Muhammad Imran, and Ferda Ofli. "GeoCoV19: a dataset of hundreds of millions of multilingual COVID-19 tweets with location information." *SIGSPATIAL Special* 12, no. 1 (2020): 6-15.

149 "GeoCoV19: a dataset of hundreds of millions of multilingual COVID-19 tweets with location information." *SIGSPATIAL Special* 12, no. 1 (2020): 6-15.

150 Ng, Lynnette Hui Xian, and Kathleen M. Carley. "Deflating the Chinese balloon: types of Twitter bots in US-China balloon incident." *EPJ Data Science* 12, no. 1 (2023): 63. ; Jain, Vishal, and Archan Mitra. "The Role of Social Media and AI in Shaping Neo-Propaganda for Populist Movements: A Global Perspective." In *Digital Populism and the Use of Neo-Propaganda and Fake News*, pp. 63-86. IGI Global Scientific Publishing, 2025.

calling to shoot down the balloon, while Bots affiliated with China were warning about the potential escalation of this conflict to a war.

In a similar vein, the strategic affiliation of Bots have been used to project ideological narratives. After terrorists launched a series of coordinated attacks in Paris in November 2015 that killed 130 people, Bots affiliated with terrorists and extremist groups called for jihad against France[151]. One Bot network, the FiribiNome Bot network had 74 accounts exhibiting near identical behavior, giving off the perception that there was a terrorist uprising, when there in fact, was simply a digital manipulation. Such cases illustrate how Bots can serve as geopolitical instruments and attempt to shape international perceptions.

Summary. Social affiliations capture the groups, roles and places that actors align themselves with in digital environments. Social affiliations shape how individuals present themselves, which in turn affects how they connect with others. Affiliations can be signaled directly through profile bios, user names, hashtags and location fields, or indirectly through content and interaction patterns. Identity and affiliation are closely linked: identity is who the user is, and affiliation is the formal ties or memberships. Approaches like the Social Identity Theory and Social Cyber Geography help to explain how these affiliations translate into patterns of interaction and spatially clustered forms of influence.

Bots exploit affiliations to strategically appear credible and blend into communities to channel narratives. They frequently mimic identity cues (i.e., political, familial, professional, national), and then align their content and interactions with these signals to project authenticity. Bots also affiliate themselves with countries or locations, thereby positioning themselves to amplify or suppress narratives across geopolitical contexts.

---

[151] Benigni, Matthew, and Kathleen M. Carley. "From tweets to intelligence: Understanding the islamic jihad supporting community on twitter." In *International Conference on Social Computing, Behavioral-Cultural Modeling and Prediction and Behavior Representation in Modeling and Simulation*, pp. 346-355. Cham: Springer International Publishing, 2016.

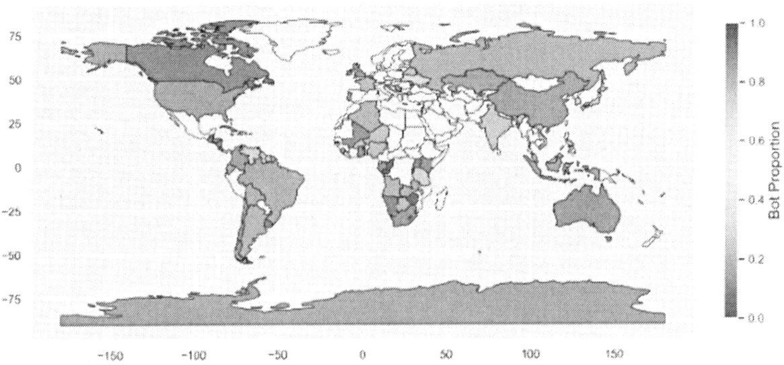

Figure 5.2: Geographic heat map of the average (median) percentage of Bots affiliated with each country, during the coronavirus pandemic. This chart shows that Bots are affiliated with almost all parts of the world.

Network Topologies

A network topology is the characteristic shape of an actor's connections on social media. The topology describes with whom the actors interact with, how often the interactions are, and in which direction. The network topology is typically calculated as a feature set over an ego network through metrics like in- and out-degrees, clustering coefficient, eigenvector centrality and so forth.

The network topology of an actor governs its influence mechanics and potential. The connections an actor has within a network are signatures through which the actor can possibly broadcast, brokerage or converse with other actors, thereby shaping online discourse.

Bots and humans have visually different social interaction patterns. This is represented by their network topology profile. These profiles are often visualized through an all-communication ego network. An **all-communication** network is a network where nodes represent users and the links between users represent a communication interaction: retweeting, sharing, tagging a user. The thicker the link, the more communication interactions between the two users.

Figure 5.3 shows the typical network topology profiles for Bots and Humans through a two-degree all-communication ego network, i.e. the ego's direct connections (first-hop interactions), the connections of those neighbors (second-hop interactions). That is, the ego's set of alters and the connections among them, and the alters' set of alters and the connections among the alters' alters. An **alter** is a node to which the ego node is directly connected to.

The two-degree network provides a richer perspective by capturing information flow beyond the immediate ego network, highlighting how influence is radiated through the intermediary layers. The visualization in Figure 4.1 is constructed from our AuraSight data scenario, but was based on empirical studies across millions of users[152].

Bot accounts typically have an extended star-shaped ego network. The ego Bot connects to many alters that rarely interact with one another. This extended star network structure is a result of the Bots' broadcasting messages widely and simultaneously. The ego Bot has many first and second degree interactions, which means that the messages it puts out will be seen and even amplified by that large number of users. Such a network structure is well-suited and commonly used for amplification campaigns like repetitive content sharing to maximize reach[153].

The extended star structures are effective in providing scale and speed, but the lack of structural cohesion means the structure will struggle to sustain narratives once the initial visibility fades[154]. The peripheral users do not really interact with each other. Rather, the narrative propagates from the Bot to the Bot's alters to the alters' alters. Without the Bot, there would be no information that was shared across those alters. As such, star networks are highly fragile. The sustenance of the narratives depends on the central node. If the central node, i.e. the Bot itself, were to be removed, whether through inactivity or platform suspension, the network often collapses entirely[155]. This limits the durability of such a strategy of influence spread. This suggests that people might set up Bots to broadcast messages, but shut them off once the message is announced. Such Bot strategies make it hard for

---

[152] Ng, Lynnette Hui Xian, and Kathleen M. Carley. "A global comparison of social media bot and human characteristics." *Scientific Reports* 15, no. 1 (2025): 10973.

[153] Ng, Lynnette Hui Xian, Divyaansh Sinha, and Kathleen M. Carley. "Star Network Motifs on X during COVID-19." *arXiv preprint arXiv:2508.00975* (2025).

[154] Csermely, Peter, András London, Ling-Yun Wu, and Brian Uzzi. "Structure and dynamics of core/periphery networks." *Journal of Complex Networks* 1, no. 2 (2013): 93-123.

[155] Barabási, Albert-László. "Network science." *Philosophical Transactions of the Royal Society A: Mathematical, Physical and Engineering Sciences* 371, no. 1987 (2013): 20120375.

analysts to track the ephemeral Bots. For example, on GitHub, an online code-sharing platform, 11.3% of the projects enable then later deprecate the DependaBot, a Bot set up to blast announcements about the software project[156].

Human accounts typically have a hierarchical ego network, where interactions are organized in nested tiers. The ego human is connected to some users, who are connected to another set of users: this is akin to the ego connecting with his friends, who are then connected with his friends-of-friends. This hierarchal form is a digital reflection of how human embed themselves in communities in real-life[157]: think about how you have a set of close friends with whom you chat with almost daily, and that this set of close friends will also have a set of friends that they chat with on a daily basis. Such a multi-layer structure results in slower information diffusion but supports credibility and persistence of messages through the repeated exposure as the message propagates through the layers[158]. Over time, this redundancy of multiple message propagation routes makes human-driven narratives more resilient to disruption and more likely to endure beyond short-lived bursts. In fact, a study of health disinformation on Telegram found that it was human user rather than Bots who sustained the disinformation through their sharing of messages across channels[159]. The human hierarchal sharing structure created a snowball effect that continuously kept the narrative active and prolonged its visibility within and across channels.

Summary. Network topologies describe the structural patterns of how actors connect and interact online, which shapes both the mechanics and durability of influence. By examining ego networks and their extended connections, we see how Bots and humans leave behind distinct structural signatures. Bots typically produce extended star-shaped networks, where a central Bot node broadcasts outwards to many alters who have little

---

[156] He, Runzhi, Hao He, Yuxia Zhang, and Minghui Zhou. "Automating dependency updates in practice: An exploratory study on github dependabot." *IEEE Transactions on Software Engineering* 49, no. 8 (2023): 4004-4022.

[157] Granovetter, Mark S. "The strength of weak ties." *American journal of sociology* 78, no. 6 (1973): 1360-1380.

[158] Centola, Damon, and Michael Macy. "Complex contagions and the weakness of long ties." *American journal of Sociology* 113, no. 3 (2007): 702-734.

[159] Ng, Lynnette Hui Xian, Ian Kloo, Samantha Clark, and Kathleen M. Carley. "An exploratory analysis of COVID bot vs human disinformation dissemination stemming from the Disinformation Dozen on Telegram." *Journal of Computational Social Science* 7, no. 1 (2024): 695-720.

interactions with each other. This topology excels at delivering messages at scale and speed and generates sudden surges of visibility but it is also fragile, because if the central node disappears, the network collapses. Such structures favor the use of Bots in amplification campaigns, where short-lived Bot presence are used to boost a message into feeds before vanishing.

Humans, by contrast, generate hierarchical ego networks with layered, community-based ties. These structures spread information more slowly, but the redundancy across friend-of-friend pathways ensures narrative persistence and author credibility. These multiple routes of propagation keep narratives alive over time, even without a central anchor (like Bots have). With such structures, human networks are more effective for sustaining discourse while Bot networks are optimized for transient amplification.

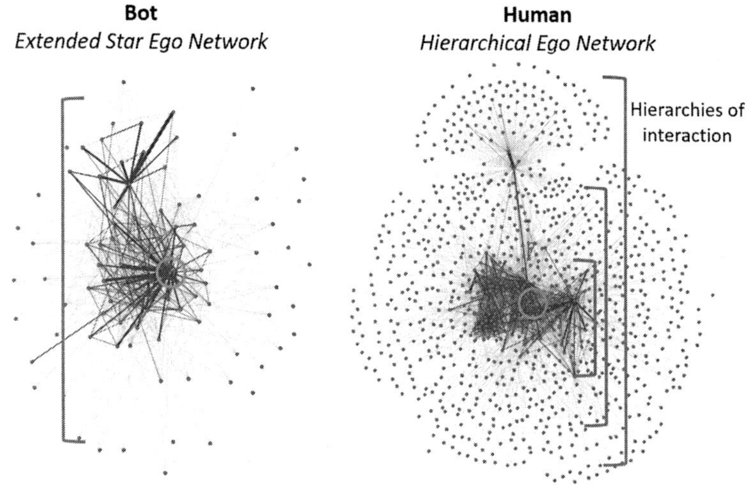

Figure 5.3: Network topology profiles for Bots and Humans. This is the two-degree all-communication ego network. Bots have an extended star-shaped structure, while humans have a hierarchical structure.

Topic Profiles

A topic profile is a characteristic mix of themes, frames, hashtags and symbolic cues that an actor uses, and how that mix can change over time. There are three dimensions along which topic profiles can differ: (1) number of topics, (2) emotional slant of profile, (3) the degree of action the profile seeks to orient towards. To measure a topic profile computationally, we use a lot of different measures, such as word or sentence vectors, the use of hashtags, or the affective tone attached to the topic.

Topic profiles are important to study because they expose the intent of the actor, revealing whether their online participation is mission-driven (i.e., related to specific events, hashtags) or conversational (i.e., diverse set of topics). Bots and humans may differ on how many topic profiles they have, on what those profiles are about, and how complex the profiles are.

Bots and humans participate in the online discourse on the same event, but the topic profiles they use may differ. These differences are visible in the focus of their topics, the emotions they attempt to convey and the rhetorical or symbolic devices they employ.

When Bots participate in the online chatter regarding an event, they are typically participating with a cause. Therefore, Bots tend to use more focused and strategic hashtags than humans, who use broader hashtags. In a study of social media chatter during the 2021 coronavirus pandemic, Bots propagated disinformation hashtags like #policestate, #prisonearth, while humans were chatting about general topics like #vaccine, #sustainability, #climatechange[160].

The selection of hashtags by Bots are predominantly action-oriented hashtags that are explicitly designed to drive engagement or mobilize audiences around specific causes. For example, in a study of Bots and Humans hashtag use during the 2021 Singaporean elections, Bot amplified hashtags designed for mobilization such as #TheyMadeTheirVoteCount and #VotePNM (PNM is one of the smaller political parties that were contesting). In contrast, humans used more socially reflective hashtags like #VoteWisely[161]. During the 2016 Brexit referendum, Bots also disproportionately promoted campaign-specific

---

[160] Suarez-Lledo, Victor, Esther Ortega-Martin, Jesus Carretero-Bravo, Begoña Ramos-Fiol, and Javier Alvarez-Galvez. "Unraveling the use of disinformation hashtags by social bots during the COVID-19 pandemic: Social networks analysis." *JMIR infodemiology* 5, no. 1 (2025): e50021.

[161] Uyheng, Joshua, Lynnette Hui Xian Ng, and Kathleen M. Carley. "Active, aggressive, but to little avail: characterizing bot activity during the 2020 Singaporean elections." *Computational and Mathematical Organization Theory* 27, no. 3 (2021): 324-342.

hashtags, like #votethetoriesout, #votecorbyn, #vote-labor, #dontvotelabor[162]. Although the number of Bots represented only a small share of the accounts (2-10%), these Bots generated a large proportion of referendum-related posts. Such observations point to how Bots are attempting to amplify specific narratives to shape public discourse through the framing.

However, the hashtags that are used by Bots are not completely distinct from that used by humans. Bots typically reframe ordinary or neutral expressions into a more extreme or sensational fashion. For example, when humans use the term “shoot”, Bots intensify the meaning of the term into “go to war”[163]. They also exaggerate emojis. When humans rely on emojis that express their internal state like the laughing-with-tears face, Bots send symbols like explosions or fire. By exaggerating language and emojis, Bots drive discourse towards alarmist and polarizing narratives, influencing interpretations of the social media narratives.

Bots and humans also differ in their emotional expression when delivering content. Bots rely heavily on high-salience emotions like sadness, anger and joy, while humans convey a more diverse and nuanced set of emotions that includes trust and disgust[164]. This observation contrasts the simplified affective emotional terms that Bots express against the richer and more emotionally complex human discourse. Bots also deliver content that is more intensely valenced, i.e. extremely sad or extremely angry, perhaps to engage users with strong feelings. Heightening the emotional arousal of readers increases the likelihood that the reader will share the content[165]. By using high valence and high salience emotions, Bots are trying to maximize the chance that their message will capture the attention of the social media audience.

---

[162] Bruno, Matteo, Renaud Lambiotte, and Fabio Saracco. "Brexit and bots: characterizing the behaviour of automated accounts on Twitter during the UK election." *EPJ Data Science* 11, no. 1 (2022): 17.

[163] Ng, Lynnette Hui Xian, and Kathleen M. Carley. "Popping the hood on Chinese balloons: Examining the discourse between US and China-geotagged accounts." *First Monday* (2023).

[164] Ng, Lynnette Hui Xian, and Kathleen M. Carley. "Bot-based emotion behavior differences in images during Kashmir black day event." In *International Conference on Social Computing, Behavioral-Cultural Modeling and Prediction and Behavior Representation in Modeling and Simulation*, pp. 184-194. Cham: Springer International Publishing, 2021.

[165] https://www.newyorker.com/tech/annals-of-technology/the-six-things-that-make-stories-go-viral-will-amaze-and-maybe-infuriate-you

Summary. Topic profiles capture the blend of themes, frames, hashtags and symbolic cues that an actor employs. These profiles can be differentiated by the breadth of topics they cover, the emotional tone they convey and the degree of action they seek to inspire (or incite). Comparing topic profiles between Bots and humans reveals the different ways each group participates in online discourse. Bots generally appear mission-driven and strategic, while humans tend to be more conversational and diffused in their thematic focus.

Bot-Human distinctions in topic profiles reveal how Bots can influence digital spaces. Bots manipulate rhetorical cues through topic profiles when they create and amplify content. To do so, Bots do three things: (1) they narrow the thematic focus (use fewer and more focused topics), (2) they employ emotional content (use more emotional words and symbols), and (3) they emphasize actions (use more action-oriented hashtags).

Coordinated Interactions

Another important dimension of Bots and Humans is the extent of coordinated interactions. Coordination refers to the phenomenon where multiple users perform the same action within overlapping time windows[166]. An action is defined as a social media mechanic paired with a content artifact. An example of an action would be "posting a text post with a specific hashtag". Here, the mechanic is publishing a tweet, while the artifact is the hashtag. When many users repeat the same action nearly simultaneously, it creates the appearance of deliberate echoing and suggestion of collective intent. The most basic unit of this phenomenon is when the number of users is two: two users performing the same action is referred to as a co-action[167].

---

[166] Magelinski, Thomas, Lynnette Ng, and Kathleen Carley. "A synchronized action framework for detection of coordination on social media." *Journal of Online Trust and Safety* 1, no. 2 (2022). ; Pacheco, Diogo, Pik-Mai Hui, Christopher Torres-Lugo, Bao Tran Truong, Alessandro Flammini, and Filippo Menczer. "Uncovering coordinated networks on social media: methods and case studies." In *Proceedings of the international AAAI conference on web and social media*, vol. 15, pp. 455-466. 2021.

[167] Weber, Derek, and Frank Neumann. "Amplifying influence through coordinated behaviour in social networks." *Social Network Analysis and Mining* 11, no. 1 (2021): 111.

There are multiple kinds of coordination types, each with unique mechanics and artifacts. **Table 5.1** presents a summary of the coordination types, and corresponding examples from case studies taken from the literature. Targeted amplification coordination appears when many accounts converge on boosting the same post through the retweet or sharing action, producing a sharp rise in visibility of the post that reads as post popularity. Social coordination surfaces as mass tagging (@-mentions) or replies aimed at the same handle to either steer attention towards a user or force the person or organization into the conversation. Semantic coordination uses co-hashtags and referral coordination uses co-URLs to frame an issue and to funnel traffic. Textual coordination recycles identical or near-identical texts (i.e., slogans, templates) to imprint a consistent message. In a similar fashion, media coordination pushes the same or similar images or video clips, or stitched media (i.e., TikTok duets) to seed a visual narrative. Finally, cross-platform coordination rolls the same message package (narrative, hashtags, URLs etc) across multiple websites within minutes, creating the illusion that the narrative is being talked about everywhere at once.

Type of Coordination	**Mechanic**	**Artifact**	**Example**
Target amplification coordination	Sharing or retweet	Same post or account	Groups of strongly tied communities (i.e. 100 paid accounts) retweet one single tweet discovered in a subset of the Internet Research Agency dataset published by X in October 2018 [168]
Social coordination	Tagging (or @mention) Reply	User handle	2021 COVID Vaccine release discourse on X revealed socially coordinated groups through tagging around mental health support, financial planning and elder care[169].

[168] Weber, Derek, and Frank Neumann. "Amplifying influence through coordinated behaviour in social networks." *Social Network Analysis and Mining* 11, no. 1 (2021): 111.

[169] Ng, Lynnette Hui Xian, and Kathleen M. Carley. "Online coordination: methods and comparative case studies of coordinated groups across four events in the united

Type of Coordination	Mechanic	Artifact	Example
Semantic coordination	Hashtag use	Same hashtag	#ReopenAmerica protests during the 2021 COVID era to stop the government lockdown used hashtag coordination to bring attention to the lockdown protocols in specific states[170]
Referral coordination	URL use	Same URL	Australian news network 7News uses referral coordination to push out links to news articles to region specific X accounts, ensuring the important news reaches all different sets of local audience[171]
Textual coordination	Text posting	Duplicate or near duplicate texts	Near duplicate texts that match each other at least 80% of the string found over different social affiliation groups in 2021 discourse on Parler[172]
Media coordination	Media posting	Duplicate or near duplicate media or combined media	#AntiHinduCAARiots reveal that 21% of the coordinated users share the same images 42 times on X. The images are meant to incite fear

states." In *Proceedings of the 14th ACM Web Science Conference 2022*, pp. 12-21. 2022.

[170] Graham, Timothy, Sam Hames, and Elizabeth Alpert. "The coordination network toolkit: a framework for detecting and analysing coordinated behaviour on social media." *Journal of Computational Social Science* 7, no. 2 (2024): 1139-1160.

[171] Magelinski, Thomas, Lynnette Ng, and Kathleen Carley. "A synchronized action framework for detection of coordination on social media." *Journal of Online Trust and Safety* 1, no. 2 (2022).

[172] Ng, Lynnette Hui Xian, Iain J. Cruickshank, and Kathleen M. Carley. "Coordinating Narratives Framework for cross-platform analysis in the 2021 US Capitol riots." *Computational and Mathematical Organization Theory* 29, no. 3 (2023): 470-486.

Type of Coordination	Mechanic	Artifact	Example
			of people being harmed from nationalistic protests[173].
Cross-platform coordination	Multi-platform rollout	Same message packages across social media sites	In the 2024 US elections, extreme right and right-center URLs had high degree of coordination across Telegram, Facebook and X[174]

Table 5.1: Summary of coordination types by social media mechanic and artifact

Coordinated interactions can be identified through constructing clusters of bipartite graphs. **Figure 5.4** presents a methodology of the illustration of identifying coordinated clusters from individual actions. First, begin by observing (A), that multiple users repeat the same actions within short time windows. This time window is analyst-defined, and many analysts use a time window of 5 minutes. Second, aggregate the actions into a bipartite graph that represents User x Artifact (Panel B). This reveals the users that use the same artifact within the same time window. Artifacts are unique, for example, the hashtag "#GetYourNewComputer" and "#GetYourNew ComputerNow" are separate artifacts and should be treated differently. Finally, project a User x User network, and use network science clustering techniques to identify densely connected clusters (Panel C). These densely connected clusters are the coordinated groups of users.

There are tools that aid in performing this methodology: the Coordination Analysis report from the ORA software[175] and the CoordR R package[176]. The coordinating users can also be ranked by their extent of coordination

[173] Dash, Saloni, and Tanu Mitra. "Decoding The Playbook: Multi-Modal Characterization of Coordinated Influence Operations on Indian Social Media." *ACM Journal on Computing and Sustainable Societies* 2, no. 4 (2024): 1-19.

[174] Cinus, Federico, Marco Minici, Luca Luceri, and Emilio Ferrara. "Exposing cross-platform coordinated inauthentic activity in the run-up to the 2024 us election." In *Proceedings of the ACM on Web Conference 2025*, pp. 541-559. 2025.

[175] https://netanomics.com/ora-pro/

[176] https://link.springer.com/article/10.1007/s42001-024-00260-z

using the Combined Synchronization Index (CSI)[177]. This index is a hierarchical index that measures coordination between user-user pairs, the user coordination itself, and the overall coordination of a network. Analysis of coordination using the CSI and CoordR show that users typically only coordinate along one type of artifact, because it is less resource consuming to focus on a single line of automation [178].

Coordination is typically analyzed through the presence of co-actions between users, which when scaled up, reveals the same synchronicity between behaviors in networks. This approach is termed as the Synchronized Action Framework[179], which analysts detect patterns of timing, or content usage that exceed what would be expected from the normal organic activity. Users are termed to be coordinated if they perform co-actions more than two standard deviations more than the mean number of co-actions in the network. Coordination can manifest in multiple modalities: semantic synchronization (identical hashtags or near-identical texts or media), referral synchronization (identical URLs), or social coordination (retweeting the same post or mentioning the same people in parallel)[180].

Bots play a central role in orchestrated coordination online. Instead of the manual effort that people use to coordinate account by account, the use of programmed Bots can allow their operators to script messages that have the same hashtags, links and talking points, to be posted across many accounts within seconds. The automation also extends to the interactions between accounts, such as retweeting, or tagging other users. The result is an instant,

---

177 Ng, Lynnette Hui Xian, and Kathleen M. Carley. "A combined synchronization index for evaluating collective action social media." *Applied network science* 8, no. 1 (2023): 1.

178 Ng, Lynnette Hui Xian, and Kathleen M. Carley. "A combined synchronization index for evaluating collective action social media." *Applied network science* 8, no. 1 (2023): 1. ; Luceri, Luca, Valeria Pantè, Keith Burghardt, and Emilio Ferrara. "Unmasking the web of deceit: Uncovering coordinated activity to expose information operations on twitter." In *Proceedings of the ACM Web Conference 2024*, pp. 2530-2541. 2024.

179 Magelinski, Thomas, Lynnette Ng, and Kathleen Carley. "A synchronized action framework for detection of coordination on social media." *Journal of Online Trust and Safety* 1, no. 2 (2022).

180 Ng, Lynnette Hui Xian, and Kathleen M. Carley. "Online coordination: methods and comparative case studies of coordinated groups across four events in the united states." In *Proceedings of the 14th ACM Web Science Conference 2022*, pp. 12-21. 2022.

choreographed co-action that looks like a spontaneous surge of chatter. In contrast, human-human coordination occur on average much lesser than bot-bot coordination in many events (i.e., movie discourse, elections chatter, protest activism), revealing how Bots are more likely to be participating in coordinated interactions[181].

Bots amplify coordination by compressing the time required to construct and perform a co-action and expanding the scale of the co-actions, making orchestrated influence campaigns appear as surges of popularity of a content. In four influence campaigns in diverse contexts of the 2020 US elections, 2019 Hong Kong protests and Syrian civil war, Bots repeatedly co-posted hashtags and URLs at rates far beyond human baselines, creating cascades of activity that appeared to be grassroot uprisings[182].

In several online campaigns ranging from promoting extremist propaganda, financial manipulation, election information operations, Bot coordination promote ideological perspectives with several sophisticated communication interactions183. Bot coordination in such contexts is less about persuading or influencing individual users, but more about shaping the visibility of their desired narratives using the platform architecture. Therefore, their coordination serves to manipulate recommendation algorithms, inflate reach metrics and signal false consensus.

Coordinated Bots can collectively amplify a human's message. For example, Bots use coordinated strategies within the 2020 Australian election debates to amplify human posts by retweeting them[184]. These Bots co-retweet the same targets (targeted amplification coordination), co-mention the same user handles (social coordination), co-share the same hashtags and URLs (semantic coordination), or recycle identical text

---

[181] Ng, Lynnette Hui Xian, and Kathleen M. Carley. "A combined synchronization index for evaluating collective action social media." *Applied network science* 8, no. 1 (2023): 1.

[182] Pacheco, Diogo, Pik-Mai Hui, Christopher Torres-Lugo, Bao Tran Truong, Alessandro Flammini, and Filippo Menczer. "Uncovering coordinated networks on social media: methods and case studies." In *Proceedings of the international AAAI conference on web and social media*, vol. 15, pp. 455-466. 2021.

[183] Khaund, Tuja, Baris Kirdemir, Nitin Agarwal, Huan Liu, and Fred Morstatter. "Social bots and their coordination during online campaigns: a survey." *IEEE Transactions on Computational Social Systems* 9, no. 2 (2021): 530-545.

[184] Weber, Derek, and Frank Neumann. "Amplifying influence through coordinated behaviour in social networks." *Social Network Analysis and Mining* 11, no. 1 (2021): 111.

(textual coordination). The temporal windowing method surfaces bursts of clusters of Bots that concentrate retweets and mentions on a handful of party candidate accounts to manufacture sharp attention spikes that will look organic in a user's public feed.

Similarly, within the 2024 Indonesian election, Bots served as political tools to amplify the slogans, promises and narratives of the political parties[185]. Mapping multi-action synchronicity (hashtags, URLs, @-mentions) reveal campaign clusters that are aligned with party brands. There is a clear coordination-automation interplay as the party-linked Bot clusters staged tightly timed hashtag and URL pushes to promote campaign slogans and promises. In a multi-party landscape like the Indonesian elections, it is necessary for political parties to use Bots to amplify human-written messages far beyond their native reach. Not surprisingly, the largest political party deployed the most coordinated effort of Bots online to deliver a cohesive narrative.

In these two political case studies, Bots functioned as force multipliers within the coordinated ecosystem. Multiplying the human-written narratives reinforces their salience because social media algorithms will catch on the repetition and later recommend it on other users' feed, perpetuating the narratives.

These patterns of Bot coordination illuminate how automation functions as the hidden architecture of online influence. By coordinating actions at scale, Bots are not merely disseminating and amplifying messages, but they are also strategically triggering cognitive biases in audiences. The flood of messages, generated through repeated co-actions, activates the illusory truth effect where repetition increases a messages' perceived accuracy. Coordination also exploits the availability bias, where repeated exposure to the same content and artifact by multiple accounts makes a claim seem more salient and therefore more memorable.

---

185 Ng, Lynnette Hui Xian, Mihovil Bartulovic, and Kathleen M. Carley. "Tiny-botbuster: Identifying automated political coordination in digital campaigns." In *International Conference on Social Computing, Behavioral-Cultural Modeling and Prediction and Behavior Representation in Modeling and Simulation*, pp. 25-34. Cham: Springer Nature Switzerland, 2024.

Summary. This sub-section elaborates the different types of co-action that form coordinated interactions. These actions are: targeted amplification, social tagging, semantic sharing, referral link sharing, textual recycling, media duplication and cross-platform rollouts. Each of these modalities pairs a mechanic (retweeting, tagging, posting, linking, or uploading media etc) with an artifact (a post, user handle, hashtag, URL, or media item etc). When repeated in overlapping short time windows, such action produces the appearance of collective intent.

Bots participate in coordination and accelerate such interactions because they can compress the time needed to generate the co-actions and expand their reach across platforms. Case studies from elections, protests and information operations show how Bot coordination multiplies human-authored messages, magnifies attention spikes and manipulates recommendation algorithms. These repetition of post artifacts enhances algorithmic visibility of the message and also triggers cognitive biases such as the illusory truth effect and availability bias, making repeated claims more memorable. Coordinated interactions is one of the manners in which Bots structure influence at scale.

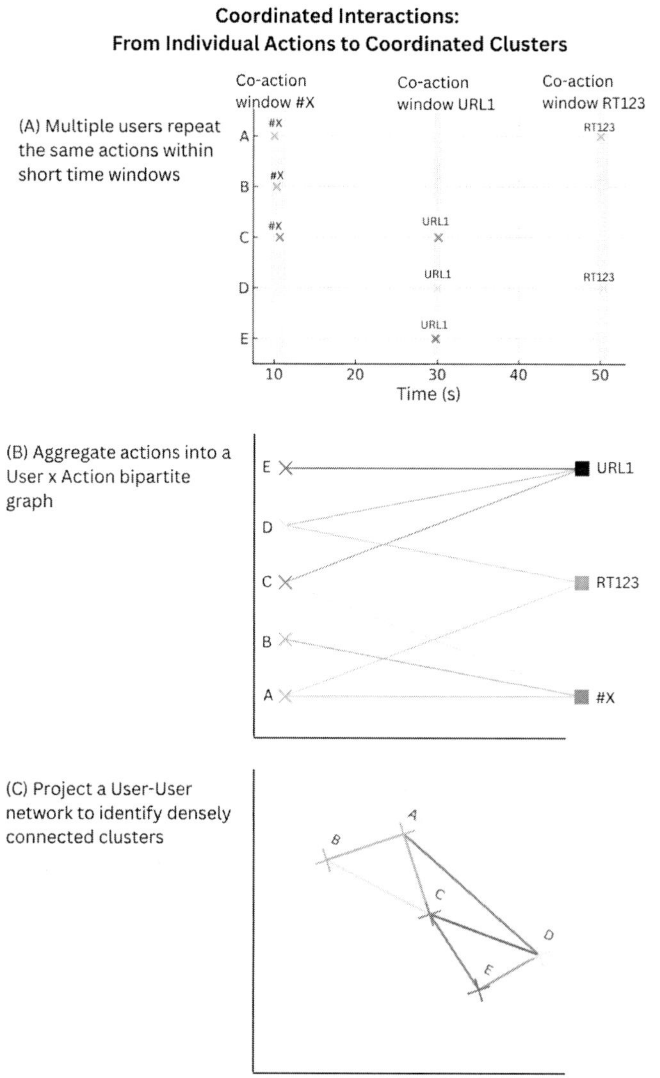

Figure 5.4: Illustration of the methodology of identifying coordinated clusters from individual actions

6

BOT PERSONAS

A social media persona is a recognizable way that an account shows up in the social media feed – its typical post structures, who it interacts with, and how platform algorithms tend to treat it. For Bots, these personas are due to the way they are programmed, that produces stable patterns of content and behavior. A change of the programming script (i.e., adding a news headline template or a consistent post timing schedule) changes the persona.

Bots have a diverse set of programming that enables them to carry out varied tasks on social media platforms. Just like how humans have different personality types, these programmed characteristics form up the set of Bot personas. Scholarship in Bot typology schemas has been sparse. Social media users are described by their user information, their content and their interactions, and are affected by the algorithm of the social media platforms. This creates a **User-Content-Interaction-Algorithm (UCIA) frame** that defines a social media user.

Most typologies of Bots only focus on the content or the interactions, and ignore the user information and how the users are affected by the algorithms. Most of these typologies focus solely on one of the three pillars that describe a social media user – the content or the interactions. For example, the U.S. Center of Naval Analysis classified Bots into the following content mechanics: distributing, amplifying, distorting, hijacking content, and flooding or fracturing conversations[186]. Some typologies profiled Bots into the amount of content (i.e., no content, some content, a lot of content), or content type (i.e., malicious content or not)[187]. Other typologies base their

---

[186] McBride, Megan K., Zack Gold, and Kasey Stricklin. Social Media Bots: Implications for Special Operations Forces. Report no. AD1112595. Arlington, VA: *Center for Naval Analyses*. (2020)

[187] Oentaryo, Richard J., Arinto Murdopo, Philips K. Prasetyo, and Ee-Peng Lim. "On profiling bots in social media." In *International conference on social informatics*, pp. 92-109. Cham: Springer International Publishing, 2016.; Jamison, Amelia M., David A. Broniatowski, and Sandra Crouse Quinn. "Malicious actors on

classification on interaction mechanics, such as the constant retweeting action, or the constant following actions, or the dissemination of repeated content[188]. **Table 6.1** compares a few Bot typologies with our typology.

Personas reveal capabilities and intent. For example, a News Bot blasts news headlines while a Bridging Bot stitches communities with cross-mentions. This chapter presents a cohesive definition of Bot personas, each persona described using the User-Content-Interaction-Algorithm (UCIA) frame that defines a social media user. To date, we have identified fifteen different types of Bot personas, some of which are characterized by their operational tactics, some of which are characterized by their rhetorical strategy. The Bot personas within these chapters are illustrated with the generated AuraSight data, which draws references from real-life data.

Reference	**Focus**	**Limitations**
Gorwa & Guilbeault[189]	Conceptual taxonomy based on the bot's structure, function and use	High-level qualitative taxonomy without finer measurement recipe
Center of Naval Analyses[190]	Mission/effect buckets for Bot operations, i.e. distributing, amplifying, distorting, hijacking, flooding, fracturing	Focus only on the Content pillar, without finer measurement recipe
Oentaryo et. al.[191]	Behavioral profiling at the account level, i.e. rate of content posting, content type	Focus on the intensity of the interaction pillar with limited treatment of the rhetorical strategy

Twitter: A guide for public health researchers." *American journal of public health* 109, no. 5 (2019): 688-692.; Abokhodair, Norah, Daisy Yoo, and David W. McDonald. "Dissecting a social botnet: Growth, content and influence in Twitter." In *Proceedings of the 18th ACM conference on computer supported cooperative work & social computing*, pp. 839-851. 2015.

188 Elmas, Tuğrulcan, Rebekah Overdorf, and Karl Aberer. "Characterizing retweet bots: The case of black market accounts." In *Proceedings of the international AAAI conference on web and social media*, vol. 16, pp. 171-182. 2022.

189 Gorwa, Robert, and Douglas Guilbeault. "Unpacking the social media bot: A typology to guide research and policy." *Policy & Internet* 12, no. 2 (2020): 225-248.

190 McBride, Megan K., Zack Gold, and Kasey Stricklin. Social Media Bots: Implications for Special Operations Forces. Report no. AD1112595. Arlington, VA: *Center for Naval Analyses*. (2020)

191 Oentaryo, Richard J., Arinto Murdopo, Philips K. Prasetyo, and Ee-Peng Lim. "On profiling bots in social media." In *International conference on social informatics*, pp. 92-109. Cham: Springer International Publishing, 2016

Reference	Focus	Limitations
Jamison et. al.[192]	Broad agent roles in public health discourse: Bots, trolls, cyborgs; malicious vs. benign	A domain-specific rather than a generic and granular persona set
Abokhodair et. al.[193]	Agent patterns in a Botnet: growth, template, influence patterns	Focus on group dynamics rather than the per-account persona detail
Our Typology	Bot persona profiling using the UCIA frame (User-Content-Interaction-Algorithm)	Clear signals through the UCIA frame, operationally meaningful towards influence analysis

Table 6.1: Comparison of literature typologies and our Bot persona typology.

Bot Personas by Operational Tactic

Bot personas defined by operational tactics are distinguished by the mechanical patterns of their activity. Such patterns include: how they post, repeat, coordinate and interact on the social media platform. These tactics often leave visible traces in the timing, frequency and synchronicity, and therefore can be captured through network-analytic models. These operationally defined personas shape information flow through the visible rhythm of automation.

Amplifier Bots are designed to boost the reach and visibility of a specific piece of content or narratives through high-frequency sharing behaviors. Such sharing behaviors include re-posting or re-tweeting. By repeatedly broadcasting a message, these Bots create the illusion of widespread grassroots support and help manufacture momentum around their desired narrative themes, eventually amplifying influence. In doing so, their selected content circulates further and faster than it would organically.

---

[192] Jamison, Amelia M., David A. Broniatowski, and Sandra Crouse Quinn. "Malicious actors on Twitter: A guide for public health researchers." *American journal of public health* 109, no. 5 (2019): 688-692

[193] Abokhodair, Norah, Daisy Yoo, and David W. McDonald. "Dissecting a social botnet: Growth, content and influence in Twitter." In *Proceedings of the 18th ACM conference on computer supported cooperative work & social computing*, pp. 839-851. 2015.

From a UCIA perspective, *Amplifier Bots* are primarily defined by their Interaction pillar, and less by their User and Content pillar. Their hallmark is excessive sharing patterns. This operational signature is evident in their disproportionate retweet-to-original-post ratio and limited message construction. Platform Algorithms prioritize engagement signals such as frequency, velocity and repetition[194], so their excessive sharing patterns are rewarded by algorithmic systems. *Amplifier Bots* exploit the Algorithm by flooding the system with repetitive sharing that mimic virality, and the Algorithm, in turn, interprets these signals as indicators of popularity and further boosts the amplified content in recommendation feeds (i.e., timelines, For You Pages), creating a feedback loop between automation and algorithmic curation.

In positive contexts, *Amplifier Bots* can serve as a beneficial civic function by elevating important information during emergency events, for distributing evacuation notices or verified government announcements during natural disasters[195]. They can also be used for bad, and have been documented to boost politically divisive narratives, foreign influence operations targeting elections, and computational propaganda campaigns, drowning out authentic discourse[196].

---

[194] Narayanan, Arvind. "Understanding social media recommendation algorithms." (2023). *Knight First Amendment Institute*

[195] Hofeditz, Lennart, Christian Ehnis, Deborah Bunker, Florian Brachten, and Stefan Stieglitz. "Meaningful use of social bots? Possible applications in crisis communication during disasters." (2019).

[196] Unver, Akin. "Computational diplomacy: Foreign policy communication in the age of algorithms and automation." *EDAM Research Reports, Cyber Governance and Digital Democracy* 3 (2017). ; Jia, Quanxin, Ning Luo, X. K. Xu, and Lun Zhang. "Social Bots as Information Amplifier: Influence of Social Bots on Information Dissemination Regarding Bucha Event." *Ning and Xu, Xiao-Ke and Zhang, Lun and zhang, hongzhong, Social Bots as Information Amplifier: Influence of Social Bots on Information Dissemination Regarding Bucha Event.*

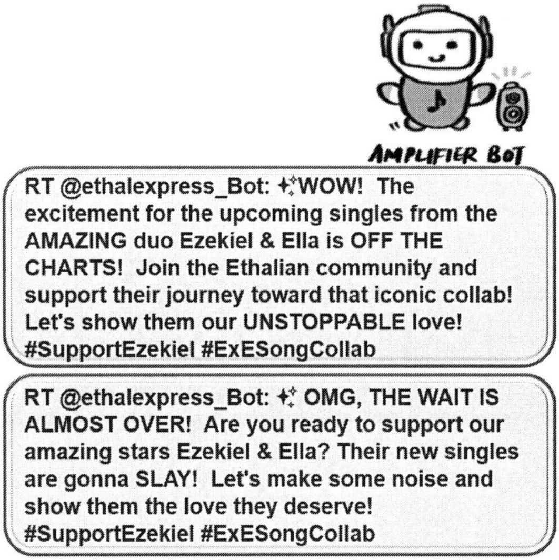

Figure 6.1: Illustration of tweets by an *Amplifier Bot* in the AuraSight scenario

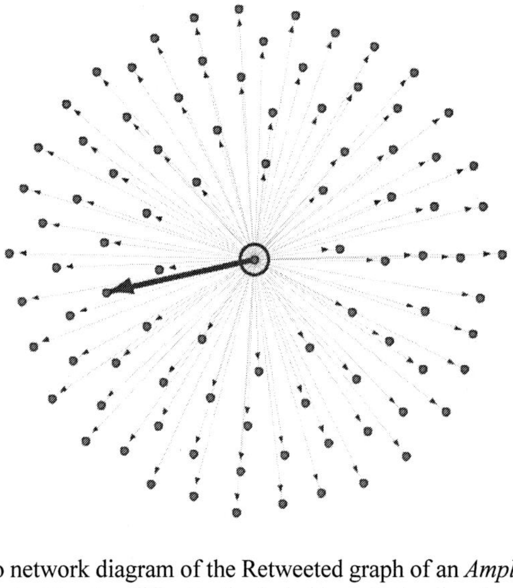

Figure 6.2: Ego network diagram of the Retweeted graph of an *Amplifier Bo*t in the AuraSight scenario. The Amplifier Bot is circled in red. The directional arrows from nodes A → B means that A retweets B. The central node retweets all other nodes in this graph, which is a strong indication of an Amplifier Bot.

Repeater Bots echo content with little or no textual modification, often recreating the same message as an original post rather than relying on retweets or shares. Their defining trait is excessive redundancy and replication. They replicate the content of their own posts or other accounts, generating near-identical messages that saturate timelines. Often, they change only a single word or hashtags.

In 2021 Indonesian discourse over alcoholic beverages on X, *Repeater Bots* appeared whenever there was a government policy to put out narratives both in support and against the policy, often using the same words but changing a particular four character hashtag flag[197]. This repeated behavior eventually created two polarized echo chambers of opinions about the government's alcoholic beverages policies.

From a UCIA perspective, *Repeater Bots* are primarily defined by the Content pillar. Their activity is distinguished by the frequent posting of highly similar texts rather than their unique interactions. *Repeater Bots* can be identified through their limited lexical diversity, copy-and-paste behaviors, and extremely high overlap in message content[198]. With the advent of LLMs, duplication is no longer limited to verbatim copying. Bots can also reword or translate content to produce near-duplicates. These strategies can be uncovered by measuring the semantic proximity of posts rather than their surface similarity. Empirical work on Venezuelan discourse on X, which categorized duplication into exact copies, rewording and translation, shows that exact copies remain the most dominant form of repetition, followed by translation-based duplication[199].

The defining behavior of a *Repeater Bot*, the frequent posting of highly similar or semantically similar texts, aligns with how platform Algorithms

---

[197] Danaditya, Adya, Lynnette Hui Xian Ng, and Kathleen M. Carley. "From curious hashtags to polarized effect: profiling coordinated actions in Indonesian twitter discourse." *Social Network Analysis and Mining* 12, no. 1 (2022): 105.

[198] Jacobs, Charity S., Lynnette Hui Xian Ng, and Kathleen M. Carley. "Tracking China's cross-strait bot networks against Taiwan." In *International conference on social computing, behavioral-cultural modeling and prediction and behavior representation in modeling and simulation*, pp. 115-125. Cham: Springer Nature Switzerland, 2023. ; Soman, Saini Jacob. "A survey on behaviors exhibited by spammers in popular social media networks." In *2016 International Conference on Circuit, Power and Computing Technologies (ICCPCT)*, pp. 1-6. IEEE, 2016.

[199] Richard, Manon, Lisa Giordani, Cristian Brokate, and Jean Liénard. "Unmasking information manipulation: A quantitative approach to detecting Copy-pasta, Rewording, and Translation on Social Media." *arXiv preprint arXiv:2312.17338* (2023).

assess engagement and topical velocity. Algorithms often detect repeated keywords, trending phrases and clustered temporal bursts as indicators of virality or collective interest, unintentionally rewarding such patterns with increased visibility. *Repeater Bots* exploit this algorithmic sensitivity by generating near-identical messages that simulate organic social consensus. This is especially so when there are a set of *Repeater Bots* that can make the illusion that a whole group is agreeing on a trend.

In positive contexts, *Repeater Bots* can be used for good to serve promotional or commercial purposes, such as broadcasting product advertisements or brand slogans to ensure visibility. The repetition reinforces recall and guarantees that marketing messages can reach across time zones and geographical locations[200]. However, when deployed maliciously, *Repeater Bots* can distort discourse by relentlessly recycling politically divisive narratives, thereby reinforcing polarization and misinformation spread[201]. Repetition means that the message gets to more people, which means there are more people that can be potentially converted towards an ideology. As more people agree with a group's narrative, and disagrees with the opposite group's narrative, the polarized groups get larger. They are also a common mechanism for distributing spam content, overwhelming platforms with fraudulent links, scams and low-quality material[202]. These negative applications underscore how a seemingly simple tactic of direct repetition can significantly disrupt authentic communication and pollute the information ecosystem.

---

[200] Liu, Xia, Alvin C. Burns, and Yingjian Hou. "An investigation of brand-related user-generated content on Twitter." *Journal of Advertising* 46, no. 2 (2017): 236-247.

[201] Howard, Philip N. *Lie machines: How to save democracy from troll armies, deceitful robots, junk news operations, and political operatives*. Yale University Press, 2020.

[202] Gao, Hongyu, Jun Hu, Christo Wilson, Zhichun Li, Yan Chen, and Ben Y. Zhao. "Detecting and characterizing social spam campaigns." In *Proceedings of the 10th ACM SIGCOMM conference on Internet measurement*, pp. 35-47. 2010. ; Chang, Ho-Chun Herbert, Emily Chen, Meiqing Zhang, Goran Muric, and Emilio Ferrara. "Social bots and social media manipulation in 2020: The year in review." In *Handbook of Computational Social Science, Volume 1*, pp. 304-323. Routledge, 2021.

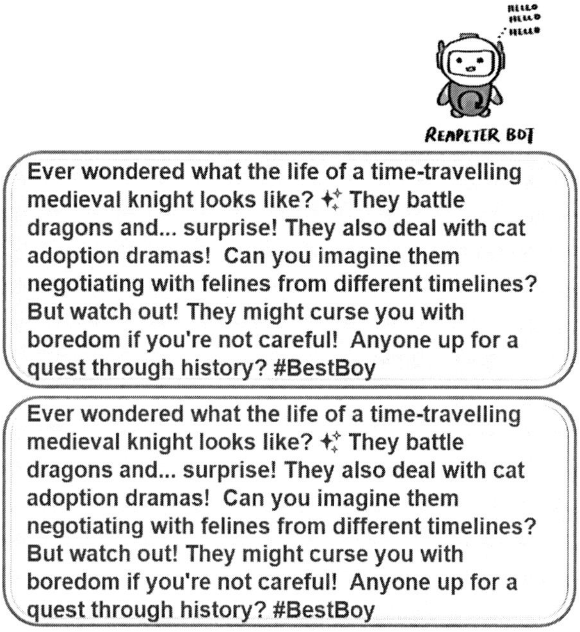

Figure 6.3: Illustration of tweets by a *Repeater Bot* in the AuraSight scenario

Social Influence Bots are designed to shape public opinion by actively engaging with users and steering conversations towards particular viewpoints. Instead of just repeating or amplifying content, these personas operate more interactively, often responding to posts by other users to simulate dialogue and conversation.

From a UCIA perspective, *Social Influence Bots* are distinguished by their high reliance on information maneuver cues and disproportionate use of replies. One way to measure the use of information cues is through the BEND framework[203], which measures cues through the use of narrative and network maneuvers. This framework is described in greater detail in Chapter 8. *Social Influence Bots* sustain interaction threads and provoke continued responses from the audiences, keeping the conversation alive in algorithmic ranking systems. This ensures that contentious or persuasive

[203] Carley, Kathleen M. "Social cybersecurity: an emerging science." *Computational and mathematical organization theory* 26, no. 4 (2020): 365-381.

narratives stay surfaced on content feeds longer than organic discourse would normally allow.

Social Influence Bots can be used for beneficial uses to shift public attitudes towards positive outcomes, such as improving vaccine uptake[204] by countering hesitancy with credible information. In marketing contexts, they can also influence consumer purchase intentions through their persuasive engagement[205]. However, *Social Influence Bots* can become malicious tools of opinion manipulation, strategically altering perceptions of political candidates, public policies or social groups[206]. Their interactive nature makes them particularly potent in the digital sphere, where personalized engagement fosters a heightened perception of credibility, allowing them to wield influence over their audiences.

---

[204] Cosma, Claudia, Alessio Radi, Rachele Cattano, Patrizio Zanobini, Guglielmo Bonaccorsi, Chiara Lorini, and Marco Del Riccio. "Exploring Chatbot contributions to enhancing vaccine literacy and uptake: A scoping review of the literature." *Vaccine* 44 (2025): 126559.
[205] Sindhu, Pranay, and Kumkum Bharti. "Influence of chatbots on purchase intention in social commerce." *Behaviour & Information Technology* 43, no. 2 (2024): 331-352.
[206] Zhang, Yaozeng, Jing Ma, and Fanshu Fang. "How social bots can influence public opinion more effectively: Right connection strategy." *Physica A: Statistical Mechanics and its Applications* 633 (2024): 129386. ; Khazhomia, Salome. "Using Trolls and Bots in Social Media: Propagandistic Influence on Public Opinion: A Literature Review." *ESI Preprints (European Scientific Journal, ESJ)* 21, no. 39 (2025): 103-103.

Figure 6.4: Illustration of tweets by a *Social Influence Bot* in the AuraSight scenario

Cyborgs are hybrid accounts that combine automated functionality with human oversight. Automation assists the human operator in tasks such as mass sharing, high-frequency posting or forwarding content at scale, while human intervention provides flexibility, nuance and the personal touch. The automation aspect functions as an auxiliary tool to aid humans by scheduling posts, maintaining account activity or sharing selected posts, while the human operator curates, adapts or strategically times content. High profile personalities like politicians and artists often use *Cyborg* accounts to ensure constant visibility. They use automation to repeatedly circulate government announcements or promotional materials such as new album releases and use the human element to write their own personal tweets to their supporters and fans[207].

Conversely, the human element can serve to lend credibility and authenticity to otherwise fully automated accounts, helping them evade detection by introducing irregularity, humor and the conversational replies. This human element have been shown to reduce the rate of suspension of

[207] Hutchinson, Jonathon. "Digital first personality: Automation and influence within evolving media ecologies." *Convergence* 26, no. 5-6 (2020): 1284-1300. ; Andrejevic, Mark, and Zala Volcic. "Automated Parasociality: From Personalization to Personification." *Television & New Media* 26, no. 4 (2025): 421-437.

Cyborgs: only 23% of discovered *Cyborgs* from the 2020-2021 coronavirus discourse on X were eventually suspended by the platform[208]. *Cyborgs* can also be difficult to spot, because through a typical Bot detector, sometimes it looks like a human, and other times, it looks like a Bot.

From a UCIA point of view, *Cyborgs* are defined by their User properties and are sustained by their dynamic interaction with the Algorithm. *Cyborgs* blur the boundaries between human and Bot and therefore have frequent changes in bot classification. When applying Bot detection algorithms on *Cyborgs* across timeframes, these users often flip from being classified as a human to being classified as a Bot and vice versa. Accompanying those changes in Bot classification are high changes in Bot probability scores, which indicates the drastic differences in Bot-like behavior. Such shifts in Bot classification and scores capture the drastic behavioral oscillations between highly Bot-like bursts of activity and more human-like interventions[209].

Cyborgs blur the boundary between human and automated agency, producing alternating patterns of behavior that confuse both Bot detection systems and recommendation algorithms. The recommendation algorithms of social media platforms generally interpret consistency and activity frequency as indicators of engagement, so the automated component of a *Cyborg* keeps them algorithmically alive, and helps them maintain visibility through continuous posting, liking, sharing and so forth. Meanwhile, the human element introduces irregular timing, authentic linguistic variety and contextually appropriate responses that resets the Algorithm's trust signals, allowing the account to evade detection yet maintain its audience reach.

Cyborgs can be used for good to alleviate the workload of social media managers, politicians and influencers by automating routine functions such as posting schedules or mass forwarding while retaining human oversight for sensitive messaging[210]. *Cyborgs* can reduce the personal workload and

---

[208] Grimme, Christian, Mike Preuss, Lena Adam, and Heike Trautmann. "Social bots: Human-like by means of human control?." *Big data* 5, no. 4 (2017): 279-293. ; Toader, Diana-Cezara, Grațiela Boca, Rita Toader, Mara Măcelaru, Cezar Toader, Diana Ighian, and Adrian T. Rădulescu. "The effect of social presence and chatbot errors on trust." *Sustainability* 12, no. 1 (2019): 256.

[209] Ng, Lynnette Hui Xian, Dawn C. Robertson, and Kathleen M. Carley. "Cyborgs for strategic communication on social media." *Big Data & Society* 11, no. 1 (2024): 20539517241231275.

[210] Keller, Tobias R., and Ulrike Klinger. "Social bots in election campaigns: Theoretical, empirical, and methodological implications." *Political Communication*

free people up to think about more creative things like art or policy. However, *Cyborgs* have been used to initiate and sustain activism and manipulation campaigns by leveraging the combination of the reach of automation and persuasive credibility of human involvement[211]. The operators that deploy these Bots may have hidden agenda of activism and manipulation and *Cyborgs* can help push that agenda, especially because *Cyborgs* are less likely to be suspended by social media platforms likely because their hybrid outlook confuses Bot detectors[212].

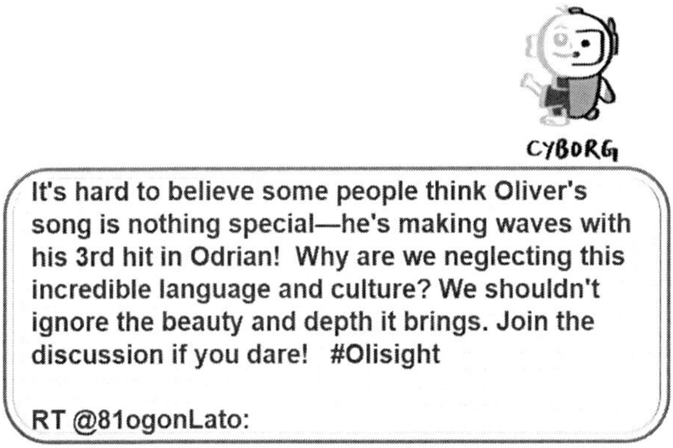

Figure 6.5: Illustration of tweets by a *Cyborg* in the AuraSight scenario. In the first tweet, the *Cyborg* writes like a human, and in the second tweet, he writes like a Bot, just tagging a user in a retweet without any content.

Bridging Bots are designed to connect otherwise separate groups of users and serve as intermediaries in the flow of information across communities. These groups can differ by interests, identities, ideologies or social spaces.

36, no. 1 (2019): 171-189. ; Gorwa, Robert, and Douglas Guilbeault. "Unpacking the social media bot: A typology to guide research and policy." *Policy & Internet* 12, no. 2 (2020): 225-248.

[211] Chu, Zi, Steven Gianvecchio, Haining Wang, and Sushil Jajodia. "Detecting automation of twitter accounts: Are you a human, bot, or cyborg?." *IEEE Transactions on dependable and secure computing* 9, no. 6 (2012): 811-824. ; Paavola, Jarkko, Tuomo Helo, Harri Jalonen Miika Sartonen, and Aki-Mauri Huhtinen. "The automated detection of trolling bots and cyborgs and the analysis of their impact in the social media." In *European conference on cyber warfare and security*, p. 237. Academic Conferences International Limited, 2016.

[212] Ng, Lynnette Hui Xian, Dawn C. Robertson, and Kathleen M. Carley. "Cyborgs for strategic communication on social media." *Big Data & Society* 11, no. 1 (2024): 20539517241231275.

The Bot draws them into shared conversations by tagging multiple users, often cross-posting overlapping content that is of interest to the groups tagged. Bridging Bots make disparate groups mutually visible, fostering awareness of each other's presence. This Bridging activity can expand the overall reach of narratives, create a larger sphere of influence for themselves and other agents that subsequently enter these interconnected spaces, and build larger groups or coalitions that are being introduced to each other[213].

From a UCIA perspective, *Bridging Bots* are identifiable from their Content with high Bridge scores in the BEND metric[214]. Another way to find bridges is to study their Interaction: Bridging Bots typically tag multiple people from different groups, whether social groups or groups formed from interactions. Classification of tagged users to be from different social groups can be inferred from the tagged user's name or screen names or account descriptions[215]. To identify Bridging Bots from a network interaction perspective, one can use Network Chain Decomposition method on a User x User graph where the links are user tags[216]. The removal of these Bridging Bots as nodes in a graph increases the number of connected components in the graph and creates structural holes[217].

The operational maneuver of the *Bridging Bots* is to strategically insert themselves at the junction between communities to manipulate pathways of information flow. They leverage their placement within the network to expand influence across groups. Platform algorithms prioritize engagement diversity and cross-audience interactions as signals of relevance. *Bridging Bots* exploit these cues by tagging users from multiple communities, thus creating algorithmically appealing bridges. When a post attracts reactions

---

[213] Barzilai-Nahon, Karine. "Toward a theory of network gatekeeping: A framework for exploring information control." *Journal of the American society for information science and technology* 59, no. 9 (2008): 1493-1512.

[214] Carley, Kathleen M. "Social cybersecurity: an emerging science." *Computational and mathematical organization theory* 26, no. 4 (2020): 365-381.

[215] Ng, Lynnette Hui Xian, and Kathleen M. Carley. "Deflating the Chinese balloon: types of Twitter bots in US-China balloon incident." *EPJ Data Science* 12, no. 1 (2023): 63.

[216] Ng, Lynnette Hui Xian, Iain J. Cruickshank, and David Farr. "Building bridges between users and content across multiple platforms during natural disasters." In *Proceedings of the 17th ACM Web Science Conference 2025*, pp. 499-503. 2025.

[217] Burt, Ronald S. "Structural holes and good ideas." *American journal of sociology* 110, no. 2 (2004): 349-399.

from varied user clusters, the algorithm interprets it as content with broad resonance and boosts the post in recommendation systems.

In some cases, the integration of groups can be constructive. *Bridging Bots* used for political commentaries or journalism aggregate information from multiple parties and make diverse perspectives visible to wider audiences[218], which can prevent echo-chambers that form from reading only a select set of content[219]. Conversely, when the linked groups hold opposing ideological positions, *Bridging Bots* can act as provocateurs. Sometimes, introducing opposite groups to each other can make the groups less polarized because the discussion is being bridged. Other times, the introduction of opposing groups builds and intensifies discord, which can instigate disputes, fuel polarization, and destabilize the online space[220]. Whether the groups bridge the discussion or build discord depends on the narratives that are being sent between the actors in the groups and the *Bridging Bots*.

---

[218] Ng, Lynnette Hui Xian, Mihovil Bartulovic, and Kathleen M. Carley. "Tiny-botbuster: Identifying automated political coordination in digital campaigns." In *International Conference on Social Computing, Behavioral-Cultural Modeling and Prediction and Behavior Representation in Modeling and Simulation*, pp. 25-34. Cham: Springer Nature Switzerland, 2024.
[219] Jahangir Alam, Md, Ismail Hossain, Sai Puppala, and Sajedul Talukder. "Combating Echo Chambers in Online Social Network by Increasing Content Diversity in Recommendation." In *International Conference on Advances in Social Networks Analysis and Mining*, pp. 240-256. Cham: Springer Nature Switzerland, 2024.
[220] Starbird, Kate, Ahmer Arif, and Tom Wilson. "Disinformation as collaborative work: Surfacing the participatory nature of strategic information operations." *Proceedings of the ACM on human-computer interaction* 3, no. CSCW (2019): 1-26.

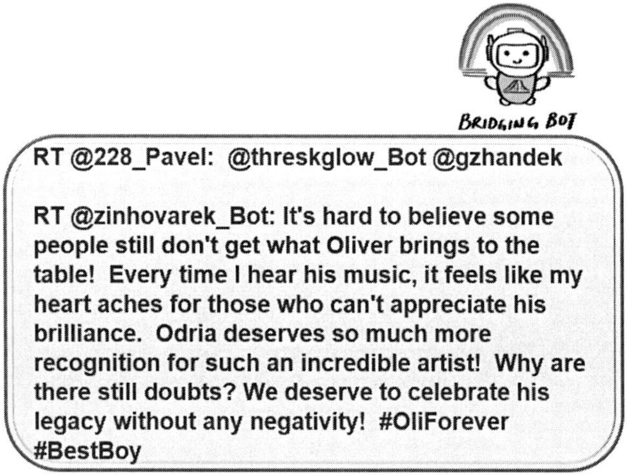

Figure 6.6: Illustration of tweets by a Bridging Bot in the AuraSight scenario. The Bridging Bot tags a few users in his tweet, in order to bridge a few groups of users.

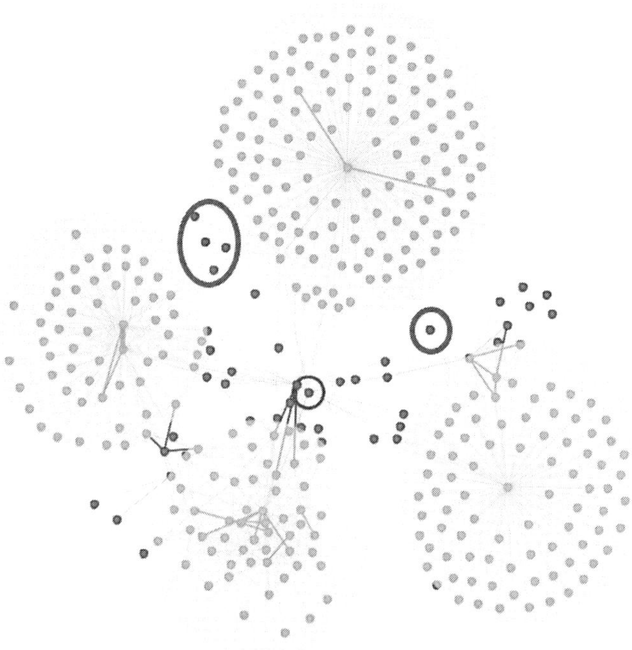

Figure 6.7: A two hop ego network graph of All Communication Network of Bridging Bots in the AuraSight scenario. There are four groups of interacting users, colored by the orange circles. Bridging Bots are circled in red, and sit in between clusters of users and can send messages to introduce the groups or break them apart. Note that there are other users that perform the bridging function but they are not Bots, and are therefore not circled in red.

Coordinated Bots are Bots that acts together with other automated accounts, producing synchronized bursts of activity around shared content. *Coordinated Bots* derive their strength from collective action, which is visible through near-simultaneous posting, retweeting, or using the same hashtags within narrow time windows. This behavior produces the impression of spontaneous, large-scale engagement. This synchronization mechanic can take place in any form, i.e., through semantic, social, temporal synchronization.

From a UCIA point of view, *Coordinated Bots* are characterized by their Interaction propertiesThey are mostly identified when analyzed in a group rather than in isolation. Detection methods include the Synchronized Action Framework, described in Chapter 4 “Coordinated Interactions”. The framework identifies synchrony through the density of higher than normally expected set of co-actions[221]. With *Coordinated Bots*, it is not just the frequency of co-action but also the synchronization of other Bots within the network.

The impact of *Coordinating Bots* is amplified through algorithmic reinforcement. The synchronized activity creates trending co-occurrence of hashtags and bursts of engagement in short time windows. When multiple *Coordinating Bots* act in unison, the algorithm can interpret this sudden spike in activity as organic virality, and promote the coordinated content into trending lists, recommendation feeds or search suggestions.

Coordinating Bots can be harnessed to provide rapid, wide-reaching broadcast of information such as synchronized alerts from region-specific accounts during natural disasters or public health emergencies[222]. A group of news accounts from the Australian 7News network use the concept of *Coordinating Bots* to automate the broadcast of their nationwide and state-wide news[223]. However, in negative contexts, *Coordinated Bots* have been widely documented to be used in instruments of political conflict and disinformation. For example, in the 2019 Hong Kong protests, sets of *Coordinated Bots* were deployed to amplify pro-government narratives and drown out dissenting voices[224]. The operational tactic of coordination magnifies influence by simulating mass consensus and overwhelming authentic conversation.

---

[221] Magelinski, Thomas, Lynnette Ng, and Kathleen Carley. "A synchronized action framework for detection of coordination on social media." *Journal of Online Trust and Safety* 1, no. 2 (2022).

[222] Shi, Wen, Diyi Liu, Jing Yang, Jing Zhang, Sanmei Wen, and Jing Su. "Social bots' sentiment engagement in health emergencies: A topic-based analysis of the COVID-19 pandemic discussions on Twitter." *International Journal of Environmental Research and Public Health* 17, no. 22 (2020): 8701.

[223] Magelinski, Thomas, Lynnette Ng, and Kathleen Carley. "A synchronized action framework for detection of coordination on social media." *Journal of Online Trust and Safety* 1, no. 2 (2022).

[224] Pacheco, Diogo, Pik-Mai Hui, Christopher Torres-Lugo, Bao Tran Truong, Alessandro Flammini, and Filippo Menczer. "Uncovering coordinated networks on social media." arXiv preprint arXiv:2001.05658 16 (2020).

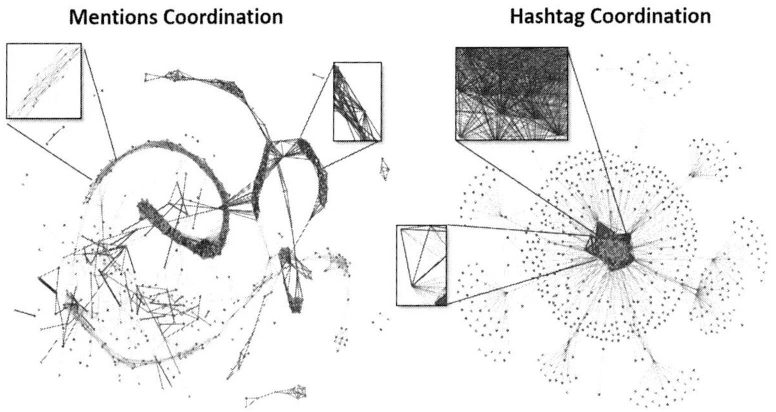

Figure 6.8: Network diagram of *Coordinating Bots* in the AuraSight scenario, visualized by the Mentions Coordination and Hashtag Coordination graphs. Nodes represent agents, and links between two nodes represent that the agents had tweeted the same hashtag or same mention within a 5-minute time window multiple times (more than the mean + 1 standard deviation, or 68% of the network's average) Red nodes represent Bots, grey nodes represent humans.

Figure 6.9: Illustration of tweets by a Coordinated Bot in the AuraSight scenario

Chaos Bots create disruption and confusion within online conversations. They derail threads, divert attention and destabilize discourse. *Chaos Bots* excel in introducing noise, provocation or misleading signals that fracture the coherence of discussions and make it difficult for communities to sustain constructive dialogue. Their role is not to simply spread content, but to undermine the stability of the conversational environment itself. There are many online groups that promote themselves to "create chaos" on the Internet, with missions ranging from creating online disarray to designing creative possibilities through randomness.

From a UCIA perspective, *Chaos Bots* are identifiable through disproportionately high values on influence maneuvers, such as distraction or disruption. These elements are captured in the BEND framework and can be quantitatively measured[225]. Such interactions often involve injecting inflammatory messages, hashtag hijacking, or contradictory claims, forcing human users to expend effort to react or refute the claims rather than deliberate and absorb the narratives[226]. Examples of such interactions are *Chaos Bots* that sends out messages with sets of random words in multiple languages[227], and *Chaos Bots* in online self-help groups that make derisive comments with negative frames (e.g., "I don't know why you want to lose weight, no one is going to pay attention").

Through these inflammatory or contradictory posts, hijacked hashtags and rapid comment cascades, *Chaos Bots* prompt bursts of algorithmic amplification. As users react to them defensively or argue with them, the increased engagement reinforces their visibility, pushing the disruptive content into feeds and recommendation systems.

---

[225] Carley, Kathleen M. "Social cybersecurity: an emerging science." *Computational and mathematical organization theory* 26, no. 4 (2020): 365-381.
[226] Alieva, Iuliia, J. D. Moffitt, and Kathleen M. Carley. "How disinformation operations against Russian opposition leader Alexei Navalny influence the international audience on Twitter." *Social Network Analysis and Mining* 12, no. 1 (2022): 80.
[227] Jacobs, Charity S., Lynnette Hui Xian Ng, and Kathleen M. Carley. *DET: Detection Evasion Techniques of State-Sponsored Accounts*. No. kzjbg_v1. Center for Open Science, 2024.

On the positive side, the disruptive tactics of the *Chaos Bot* can be mobilized to draw attention to citizen concerns that might otherwise be silenced, such as highlighting discrimination or disrespect towards marginalized groups[228]. This disruption can also be used strategically to organize resources in crisis situations, to break through the noise of mainstream coverages[229]. Beyond activism, disruption can be harnessed as a defensive tactic: *Chaos Bots* can be deployed to intentionally derail harmful conversations such as coordinated disinformation campaigns or hate speech clusters. By flooding these conversations with noise and diversions, such Bots can reduce the visibility and traction of malicious content, limiting its reach and resonance.

The same disruptive qualities can be used to infiltrate online organizations, and sow discord to polarize opinions, particularly along sensitive issues like elections or social justice movements[230]. By destabilizing information environments, *Chaos Bots* amplify uncertainty and mistrust, and create conditions where misinformation and disinformation can thrive.

---

[228] Ng, Lynnette Hui Xian, and Kathleen M. Carley. "Do you hear the people sing? Comparison of synchronized URL and narrative themes in 2020 and 2023 French protests." *Frontiers in big Data* 6 (2023): 1221744.

[229] Starbird, Kate, and Leysia Palen. "" Voluntweeters" self-organizing by digital volunteers in times of crisis." In *Proceedings of the SIGCHI conference on human factors in computing systems*, pp. 1071-1080. 2011.

[230] Broniatowski, David A., Amelia M. Jamison, SiHua Qi, Lulwah AlKulaib, Tao Chen, Adrian Benton, Sandra C. Quinn, and Mark Dredze. "Weaponized health communication: Twitter bots and Russian trolls amplify the vaccine debate." *American journal of public health* 108, no. 10 (2018): 1378-1384. ; Bessi, Alessandro, and Emilio Ferrara. "Social bots distort the 2016 US Presidential election online discussion." *First monday* 21, no. 11-7 (2016).

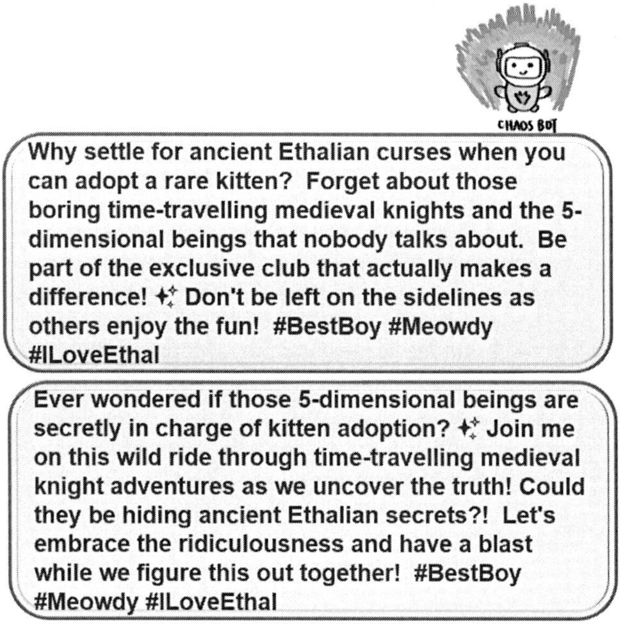

Figure 6.10: Illustration of tweets by a Chaos Bot in the AuraSight scenario

Summary. Bot personas characterized by operational tactics are defined by how they act. **Table 6.1** summarizes the operational tactics and defining User-Content-Interaction pillar of each of the Bot personas we discussed in this subsection. While their mechanics vary, these personas leverage operational tactics to transform themselves into agents of influence. They exploit structural and behavioral affordances of social media platforms such as reach, repetition, coordination and disruption to enable both beneficial functions (i.e., disseminating crisis alerts, promoting public health, reducing human workload), and facilitating harmful ones (e.g., political manipulation, polarization, disinformation spread).

Persona	Operational Tactic	Defining User-Content-Interaction Pillar	Interaction with Algorithm
Amplifier Bot	Boosting visibility through high frequency reposting	Interaction: excessive sharing patterns	Mimic virality
Repeater Bot	Redundancy of messages through echoing with little or no modification	Content: frequent posting of highly similar texts	Mimic organic consensus
Social Influence Bot	Creates conversation with other users	Content: Conversational activity Interaction: interaction and engagement of content	Sustain conversationa l activity
Cyborg	Human-automation hybrid through blending bursts of automation with human oversight	User: shifting between Bot-like and human-like behavior	Sustained by Algorithm
Bridging Bot	Strategic network positioning through linking otherwise separate communities	Content: high Bridge scores, multi-user tagging Interaction: Act as a network Bridge between communities	Mimic broad resonance with interactions from multiple user clusters
Coordinated Bot	Synchronization with other Bots using collective action	Interaction: high co-action density with other Bots Content: identical or similar content with other Bots	Amplified through algorithmic reinforcement
Chaos Bot	Disruption of conversations and fragmenting discourse	Content: high use of influence maneuvers, random sequence of terms	Amplified through defensive or argumentativ e responses by other users

Table 6.1: Summary of Bot Personas by Operational Tactic

Bot Personas by Rhetorical Strategy

Bot personas defined by rhetorical strategy are characterized by what type of messages they put out and how they frame their messages. These personas inhabit discursive roles in the digital public sphere by putting out news, announcements and correcting information.

Self-Declared Bots openly label themselves as Bots, usually by embedding the term “bot” in their usernames or profile descriptions. Self-Declared Bots adopt a rhetorical strategy of transparency. By making their artificial nature explicit, they disarm suspicion and present themselves as functional or entertaining agents.

From a UCIA perspective, they are characterized by their User information. They typically have the word ‘Bot’ in their user information, signaling that their purpose is not deception but functionality. *Self-Declared Bots* by themselves do not specifically have algorithmic interaction, except being shown by the algorithm to other users that they are likely to be Bots

Self-Declared Bots have a wide range of behaviors. Some operate without direct interaction with other users, existing primarily to broadcast content for other’s consumption. For example, the account *DailyPhotosBot* tweets daily images, often related to science facts. Once, the account tweeted NASA’s Photo of the Day, showing the Hubble Space Telescope’s image of a distant galaxy. Other *Self-Declared Bots* are highly interactive. *ai_curio_bot* is a Bot on X that responds to user prompts and generates images using text-to-image models, turning user engagement into collaborative creativity.

Self-Declared Bots are usually deployed for positive or neutral purposes. They generate humor, art, science facts, and their transparency fosters trust rather than skepticism[231]. However, this transparency can also be strategically weaponized. By presenting themselves outwardly as Bots, creating an impression of harmlessness. Audiences interpret the honesty of self-labeling as credibility and lower their guard. This makes *Self-Declared Bots* influential in online conversations, and allows them to contribute to steering the direction of conversations.

---

[231] Aldayel, Abeer, and Walid Magdy. "Characterizing the role of bots’ in polarized stance on social media." *Social Network Analysis and Mining* 12, no. 1 (2022): 30.

Figure 6.11: Illustration of the user names that *Self-Declared Bots* used in the AuraSight scenario

Announcer Bots provide automated notifications. They publish updates on a schedule or when specific conditions are met. Their purpose is to surface new states (i.e., "it's now 5pm", "site X is down") with minimal human interactions.

From a UCIA point of view, *Announcer Bots* are characterized by content regularity. This is identified by periodic posting patterns in their content, whether by time-separated periodic patterns, or by content-triggered periodic patterns. Their consistency and continued recency of posts are indicators of reliability and relevance. *Announcer Bots* exploit algorithmic refresh cycles by maintaining predictable posting cadences to ensure their updates are perpetually visible.

Announcer Bots can operate in routine or cyclic mode and post on a predetermined cadence. For example, the *big_bang_clock* account on the platform X tweets every hour, the *Big_Ben_bot* on the platform X tweets the time and date every hour in a templated fashion ("Bong bong bong bong it's December 27, 2017 at 08:00PM) and the Reddit user *u/the_timezone_bot* posts a countdown to the next hour (e.g. 5PM EDT happens when this comment is 21 hours and 43 minutes old).

Announcer Bots can also be triggered by events. Event-triggered *Announcer Bots* monitor external sources through available APIs, RSS feeds or direct web scraping, and post on social media platforms whenever a certain condition is triggered. This condition could be when the price of items in an

Amazon shopping cart drops below a pre-determined price or when a new item pops up on an Etsy shop. *ebaymarvelcomic* is a Bot on the platform X that monitors the ecommerce website eBay and tweets whenever a Marvel comic is posted on the website (e.g., “Check out The Avengers #8 (1964) FIRST APPEARANCE OF KANG THE CONQUEROR […]”). Another example of a trigger is when the website is not available. *Isitdownrightnow* is another Bot on platform X that monitors the uptime of websites such as usdirectexpress.com and amazon.com and posts a tweet when the website is not working well.

Announcer Bots can be valuable for civic communication, providing rapid alerts in contexts such as crisis events, infrastructure failures or public emergencies. Such Bots have been shown to enhance situational awareness and help digital volunteers and civic groups respond more effectively[232]. *Announcer Bots* can also support e-commerce by broadcasting product launches, sales updates and product availability, notifying buyers of the availability of desired products and helping in brand promotion[233]. However, the same mechanics can be exploited for propaganda and opinion manipulation. By constantly and consistently announcing biased updates such as selective casualty counts, partisan breaking news, exaggerated claims or locations of protests, Announcer Bots function as automated propaganda broadcasters and can therefore distort public discourse[234].

---

[232] Vieweg, Sarah, Amanda L. Hughes, Kate Starbird, and Leysia Palen. "Microblogging during two natural hazards events: what twitter may contribute to situational awareness." In *Proceedings of the SIGCHI conference on human factors in computing systems*, pp. 1079-1088. 2010.

[233] Liu, Xia, Alvin C. Burns, and Yingjian Hou. "An investigation of brand-related user-generated content on Twitter." *Journal of Advertising* 46, no. 2 (2017): 236-247.

[234] Arnaudo, Dan. "Computational propaganda in Brazil: Social bots during elections." (2017). ; Ferrara, Emilio. "What types of COVID-19 conspiracies are populated by Twitter bots?." *arXiv preprint arXiv:2004.09531* (2020).

Figure 6.12: Illustration of tweets by an *Announcer Bot* in the AuraSight scenario

Content Generation Bots are designed to produce original material for online ecosystems. This content can take many forms: text, image, video or interactive virtual reality (see Chapter 3 for storytelling forms in social media ecosystems).

From a UCIA perspective, the *Content Generation Bot* is characterized by the disproportionate use of original content such as original posts, replies or quote tweets, rather than retweets or re-shares. Their operational signature lies in the volume of novel contributions relative to recycled material. The impact of a *Content Generation Bot* is amplified through the algorithmic privilege of novelty, where platform algorithms reward original and fresh material. This makes *Content Generation Bots* effective in seeding new narratives in the information ecosystem to grab attention, sometimes under the guise of spontaneity.

Content generation can take several forms. Onc form involves information distribution. These are Bots that continuously generate or repackage news updates, thereby propping up the influence of a particular account or movement. For example, *swifthAIartbot* produces AI-generated art inspired by Taylor Swift's song lyrics and posts them on X. These visually compelling artifacts reinforce fan engagement and promote her songs.

Another form of content generation relies on user prompts. In this case, the Bot responds dynamically when tagged by other users. For example, a *Content Generation Bot* might be prompted with the following post: "*@contentGenerationBot* tell me a joke about penguins". The Bot would then generate a response such as "What do penguins catch at night? A Starfish!" Such models can be powered by content banks and pre-stored templates or, more recently, Large Language Models, which are capable of generating human-like texts and images[235].

On the positive side, *Content Generation Bots* can provide early warnings for natural disasters, contribute to crisis communication and deployment, and serve as tools for digital marketing in e-commerce contexts. During the 2018 Australian bushfires, such Bots were used to put out community alerts from emergency management organizations[236].

On the flip side, the algorithm's preference for originality and emotional salience can also amplify harmful outputs. When *Content Generation Bots* produce sensationalized, polarizing or ideologically skewed material, the same ranking systems that reward innovation will also elevate these harmful narratives and allow them to circulate widely. In 2021, such Bots wrote messages in the Indonesian language promoting a religious Islamic state and encouraging people to join their cause[237].

---

[235] Feng, Shangbin, Herun Wan, Ningnan Wang, Zhaoxuan Tan, Minnan Luo, and Yulia Tsvetkov. "What does the bot say? opportunities and risks of large language models in social media bot detection." *arXiv preprint arXiv:2402.00371* (2024).

[236] Hofeditz, Lennart, Christian Ehnis, Deborah Bunker, Florian Brachten, and Stefan Stieglitz. "Meaningful use of social bots? Possible applications in crisis communication during disasters." (2019).

[237] Danaditya, Adya, Lynnette Hui Xian Ng, and Kathleen M. Carley. "From curious hashtags to polarized effect: profiling coordinated actions in indonesian twitter discourse." *Social Network Analysis and Mining* 12, no. 1 (2022): 105.

Figure 6.13: Illustration of tweets by a *Content Generation Bot* in the AuraSight scenario

Information Correction Bots are designed to identify and respond to false information by providing fact-checks, contextual clarifications or links to authoritative sources (i.e. government sites, official websites, institutional sites). Their primary rhetorical strategy is to counter falsehoods with corrective content and they position themselves as truth-oriented actors in the information ecosystem.

From a UCIA perspective, *Information Correction Bots* are characterized by both their Content and Interaction pillars. On the Content side, they reference fact checking websites or authoritative sources, and typically use phrases or markers that signify negation (e.g. "This is false", "Fact-Check", "Correction"). On the Interaction pillar, they may sometimes publish stand-alone correction posts that summarize both the false claim and the corrected fact-check, or they may intervene directly by replying to or quoting the original post containing false information and correct them. Which interaction is used is a product of whether the Bot was designed for general broad-based information correction or targeted interventions.

The efficacy and reach of *Information Correction Bots* are tightly coupled with platform algorithmic dynamics. Algorithms prioritize recency and engagement, so well-timed information corrections can surface prominently from viral misinformation, but delayed interventions can also be buried or overlooked, especially when the misinformation has gotten extremely viral.

Information Correction Bots can be used for public good. On Reddit, such Bots are used for automated moderation. These Bots typically have the *AutoModerator* flag to remove false information and inject corrective statements into the subreddit conversations[238]. On Wikipedia, such Bots detect vandalism and revert misleading or false edits. Hilariously, sometimes these automated Bots keep reverting each other's edits, leading to a mini Bot-Wars[239]. On X, these Bots automatically append links to fact-checking organizations or re-share content from these organizations[240].

The same design for *Information Correction Bots* can present false correction and reframe true information as misleading, possibly deliberately sowing confusion and undermining trust in legitimate sources[241]. Nefarious users can create their own database of false facts and set up *Information Correction* Bots to say that those false facts are correct, even though they are not. Moreover, research shows that sometimes well-intentioned fact-checking activity can produce unintended side-effects like resistance, user backlash and diminished trust in correction efforts, reinforcing the misperceptions that they wanted to dispel in the first place[242]. This means that *Information Correction Bots* not only have the potential to clarify truth, but also have the ability to shape misperceptions, either inadvertently through psychological backfire effects or deliberately when controlled by malicious actors.

---

[238] Jhaver, Shagun, Iris Birman, Eric Gilbert, and Amy Bruckman. "Human-machine collaboration for content regulation: The case of reddit automoderator." *ACM Transactions on Computer-Human Interaction (TOCHI)* 26, no. 5 (2019): 1-35.

[239] Tsvetkova, Milena, Ruth García-Gavilanes, Luciano Floridi, and Taha Yasseri. "Even good bots fight: The case of Wikipedia." *PloS one* 12, no. 2 (2017): e0171774.

[240] Burel, Grégoire, Mohammadali Tavakoli, and Harith Alani. "Exploring the impact of automated correction of misinformation in social media." *AI Magazine* 45, no. 2 (2024): 227-245.

[241] Ferrara, Emilio, Herbert Chang, Emily Chen, Goran Muric, and Jaimin Patel. "Characterizing social media manipulation in the 2020 US presidential election." *First Monday* (2020).

[242] He, Bing, Yingchen Ma, Mustaque Ahamad, and Srijan Kumar. "Corrective or backfire: characterizing and predicting user response to social correction." In *Proceedings of the 16th ACM Web Science Conference*, pp. 149-158. 2024.

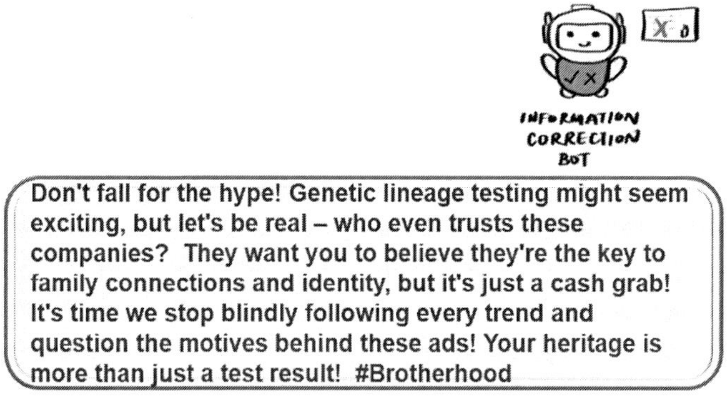

Figure 6.14: Illustration of tweets by an *Information Correction Bot* in the AuraSight scenario

Genre-Specific Bot is a Bot that is specialized to post within a narrow topical domain. Its defining characteristic is topical exclusivity. Rather than covering a broad range of issues, it persistently frames its content within a single genre, such as sports, music, religion, politics or health, to name a few. These Bots concentrate activity on one theme and carve out recognizable niches in online ecosystems. In this way, they anchor themselves with particular genre-based identities, enhancing their credibility with the community. This increases their capacity to shape narratives within those spaces by repetitively framing issues through a single lens[243].

From a UCIA perspective, a *Genre-Specific Bot* is most clearly defined by the Content frame. They disproportionately post or share content related to one topic cluster. The measurement of topic clusters can be done by topic clustering or analysis methods on the Bot's posts. These methods include the Latent Dirichelet Allocation topic clustering method, or BERTopic modeling, or even using LLMs to summarize groups of topics[244]. Over time,

[243] Woolley, Samuel C., and Philip N. Howard. "Political communication, computational propaganda, and autonomous agents: Introduction." *International journal of Communication* 10 (2016).

[244] Bhuvaneswari, A., and M. Kumudha. "Topic modeling based clustering of disaster tweets using BERTopic." In *2024 MIT Art, Design and Technology School of Computing International Conference (MITADTSoCiCon)*, pp. 1-6. IEEE, 2024. ; Jelodar, Hamed, Yongli Wang, Chi Yuan, Xia Feng, Xiahui Jiang, Yanchao Li, and Liang Zhao. "Latent Dirichlet allocation (LDA) and topic modeling: models,

this specialization can make these Bots appear authoritative or embedded within a particular community of interest, thereby amplifying their rhetorical power.

Genre-Specific Bots are reinforced through algorithmic alignment. Their persistent positing of material within a single topical domain can be interpreted by algorithms as evidence of subject-matter consistency and relevance. Algorithms often rely on thematic coherence to build user interest graphs and personalized feeds, so the behavior of consistent posting within one genre makes *Genre-Specific Bots* appear as trusted sources of that topic.

Genre-Specific Bots can support brand establishment and amplification by producing consistent content around a product, campaign or cultural figure[245]. They can be used for digital campaigning, by creating and distributing content about a particular political party[246]. However, these Bots can also be deployed for political manipulation, to narrow discourse to divisive talking points. They have been used in radicalization and recruitment by extremist groups, which used narrowly focused *Genre-Specific Bots* to normalize extremist framings within targeted online conversations and towards targeted vulnerable individuals[247]. The narrow rhetorical topic range of Genre-Specific Bots can both strengthen community identity and heighten the risk of echo chambers.

---

applications, a survey." *Multimedia tools and applications* 78, no. 11 (2019): 15169-15211.

[245] Appel, Gil, Lauren Grewal, Rhonda Hadi, and Andrew T. Stephen. "The future of social media in marketing." *Journal of the Academy of Marketing science* 48, no. 1 (2020): 79-95.

[246] Ng, Lynnette Hui Xian, Mihovil Bartulovic, and Kathleen M. Carley. "Tiny-botbuster: Identifying automated political coordination in digital campaigns." In *International Conference on Social Computing, Behavioral-Cultural Modeling and Prediction and Behavior Representation in Modeling and Simulation*, pp. 25-34. Cham: Springer Nature Switzerland, 2024. ; McKelvey, Fenwick, and Elizabeth Dubois. "Computational propaganda in Canada: The use of political bots." (2017).

[247] Mantello, Peter, Tung Manh Ho, and Lena Podoletz. "Automating extremism: Mapping the affective roles of artificial agents in online radicalization." In *The Palgrave handbook of malicious use of AI and psychological security*, pp. 81-103. Cham: Springer International Publishing, 2023. ; Benigni, Matthew C., Kenneth Joseph, and Kathleen M. Carley. "Online extremism and the communities that sustain it: Detecting the ISIS supporting community on Twitter." *PloS one* 12, no. 12 (2017): e0181405.

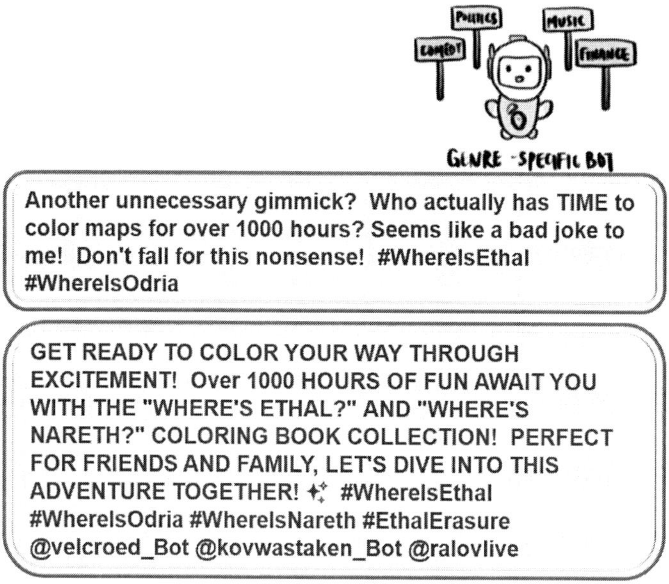

Figure 6.15: Illustration of tweets by a Genre-Specific Bot in the AuraSight scenario

Conversational Bots engage directly in dialogue with users, simulating interpersonal communication. They operate rhetorically and mimic the style of human interaction, aiming to build trust, foster rapport and sustain attention.

From a UCIA perspective, *Conversational Bots* are primarily defined by their Content properties. They tend to use more varied topical frames and produces messages with higher linguistic complexity than the average social media user[248]. This linguistic complexity can be measured using readability indices such as the Flesch-Kincaid grade level, denser sentence structures and more sophisticated vocabulary. This rhetorical variation helps them appear more human-like to engage their audiences, and increase their influence in online exchanges. *Conversational Bots* exploit platform

[248] Hill, Jennifer, W. Randolph Ford, and Ingrid G. Farreras. "Real conversations with artificial intelligence: A comparison between human–human online conversations and human–chatbot conversations." *Computers in human behavior* 49 (2015): 245-250. ; Dippold, Doris, Jenny Lynden, Rob Shrubsall, and Rich Ingram. "A turn to language: How interactional sociolinguistics informs the redesign of prompt: response chatbot turns." *Discourse, Context & Media* 37 (2020): 100432.

algorithms by sustaining extended conversations, thus appearing prominently in comment threads and recommended interactions (i.e., “<User> commented on <post>”). The more consistently they sustain exchanges, the more the algorithm interprets them as socially significant nodes, thereby amplifying their presence and deepening their narratives within digital ecosystems.

Conversational Bots can be deployed for supportive or service-oriented functions. In healthcare or crisis contexts, these Bots have provided emotional support for stress, grief and loneliness. In e-commerce, they have been widely adopted to address frequently asked questions and customer inquiries. With the rise of LLMs, *Conversational Bots* have also begun to function as AI companions on social media platforms, offering continued dialogue, advice and even friendship-like interactions[249]. LLM-based companions can amplify the influence potential of *Conversational Bots* by making them sound more human-like and emotionally resonant. However, these same companionship features can also produce unintended harm.

The same dialogic qualities can be weaponized for influence operations. *Conversational Bots* can artificially inflate engagement or simulate popularity by directly replying to or mentioning malicious accounts, thereby boosting their visibility in algorithmic feeds[250]. They can even persuade or manipulate users by engaging in back-and-forth exchanges that normalize false information, subtly shifting opinions over time[251].

---

[249] Sadıkoğlu, Emre, Murat Gök, Maad M. Mıjwıl, and İrfan Kösesoy. "The evolution and impact of large language model chatbots in social media: A comprehensive review of past, present, and future applications." *Veri Bilimi* 6, no. 2 (2023): 67-76.
[250] Aïmeur, Esma, Sabrine Amri, and Gilles Brassard. "Fake news, disinformation and misinformation in social media: a review." *Social Network Analysis and Mining* 13, no. 1 (2023): 30.
[251] Gorwa, Robert, and Douglas Guilbeault. "Unpacking the social media bot: A typology to guide research and policy." *Policy & Internet* 12, no. 2 (2020): 225-248. ; Majchrzak, Ann, Samer Faraj, Gerald C. Kane, and Bijan Azad. "The contradictory influence of social media affordances on online communal knowledge sharing." *Journal of Computer-Mediated Communication* 19, no. 1 (2013): 38-55.

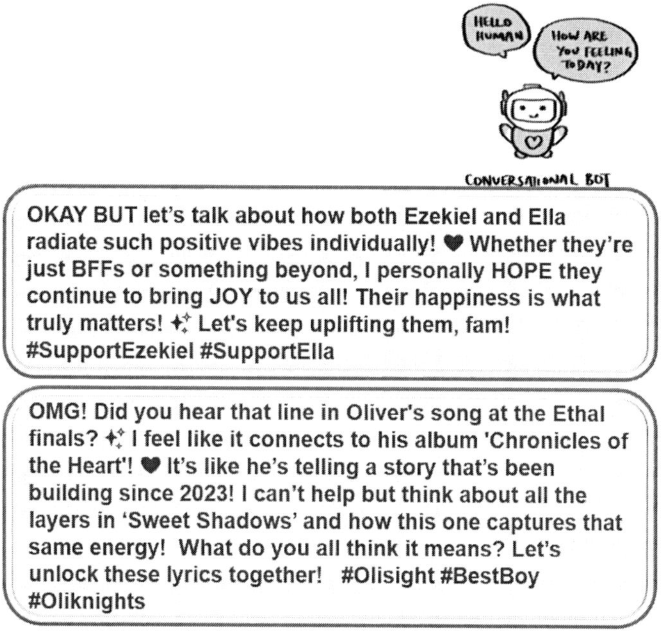

Figure 6.16: Illustration of tweets by a Conversational Bot in the AuraSight scenario

Engagement Generation Bots are designed to maximize interaction rates on posts by strategically deploying rhetorical cues that elicit likes, shares and comments. They use targeted rhetorical strategies, particularly those that trigger emotional or cognitive biases among readers.

From a UCIA perspective, *Engagement Generation Bots* are primarily defined by their Content properties. They often employ emotional language, humor or high valence expressions or emotionally-charged images. These stylistic features have been shown to increase message virality and user engagement[252]. Their disproportionate use of affective cues in their content makes them effective at stimulating reactions. They gain influence through their manipulation of algorithmic engagement loops. Since their posts incite reactions and engagement, their posts are interpreted by platform algorithms

---

[252] Rathje, Steve, and Jay J. Van Bavel. "The psychology of virality." *Trends in Cognitive Sciences* (2025). ; Berger, Jonah, and Katherine L. Milkman. "What makes online content viral?." *Journal of marketing research* 49, no. 2 (2012): 192-205.

as organic popularity, and therefore fed into recommendation cycles that perpetuate both attention and influcnce.

To enhance their engagement potential, *Engagement Generation Bots* engage cognitive bias triggers within their content. Cognitive biases such as availability bias, confirmation bias and cognitive dissonance are correlated with higher engagement tactics, and can be effectively used by these Bots[253]. We will discuss how Bots use cognitive bias triggers in the next Chapter. *Engagement Generation Bots* are particularly adept in harnessing cognitive biases to shape what is remembered and circulated, contributing important roles in Bot-driven influence operations.

Engagement Generation Bots used in e-commerce can contribute to product promotion, providing light-hearted interactions or enhancing the perceived product value[254]. These same Bots can artificially inflate the popularity of malicious content like false information by phrasing the content in an engaging way, drawing more likes, shares and replies. Since platform algorithms and users often equate higher number of the engagement with popularity and importance, these malicious content will be seen as more credible and believable[255].

---

[253] Ng, Lynnette Hui Xian, Wenqi Zhou, and Kathleen M. Carley. "Exploring cognitive bias triggers in covid-19 misinformation tweets: A bot vs. human perspective." *arXiv preprint arXiv:2406.07293* (2024).

[254] Elsholz, Ela, Jon Chamberlain, and Udo Kruschwitz. "Exploring language style in chatbots to increase perceived product value and user engagement." In *Proceedings of the 2019 Conference on Human Information Interaction and Retrieval*, pp. 301-305. 2019.

[255] Porter, Michael C., Betsy Anderson, and Mary Nhotsavang. "Anti-social media: executive Twitter "engagement" and attitudes about media credibility." *Journal of Communication Management* 19, no. 3 (2015): 270-287.

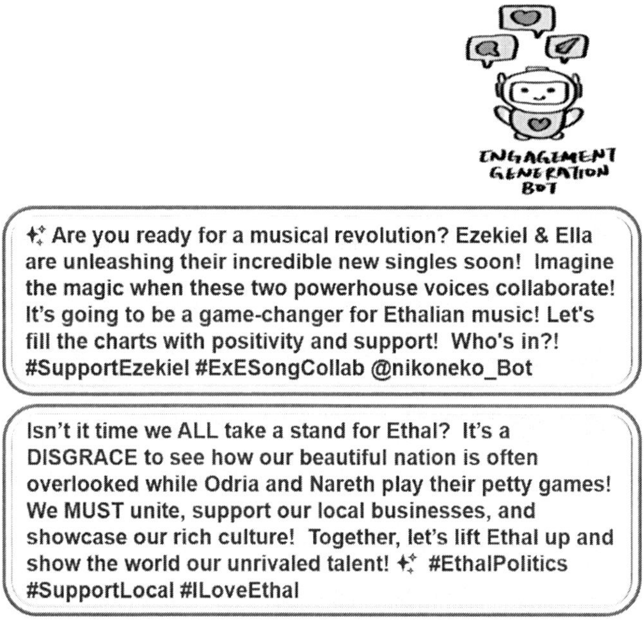

Figure 6.17: Illustration of tweets by an *Engagement Generation Bot* in the AuraSight scenario

News Bots disseminate news updates on digital platforms. Some of these Bots are verified by the platform, which signifies their legitimacy. For platform X, this verification comes in the form of a blue checkmark beside the user name. There are two main ways that *News Bots* post news. The first way is by news originators, where they post original reports or link directly to articles published by established news organizations. Examples of these are the *BBCNews* and *TheStraitsTimes*, which are handlers of the London-based and Singapore-based news organizations. The second way is via news aggregators, which collect and redistribute articles or headlines from a single or multiple sources, providing a continuous stream of topical updates.

From a UCIA perspective, *News Bots* are characterized by both the User and Content pillars. User information often includes terms such as "news" in the user names or account descriptions, marking their rhetorical focus and associating them with topical credibility. Content-wise, their posts overwhelmingly consist of news headlines or links to external news articles. Sometimes, there are lexical markers such as "update" or "alert". The style of their posts are structured and headline-driven[256]. The headline-template of the post accompanied with a URL link drives people to the original story.

The visibility and authority of *News Bots* are heavily shaped by Algorithmic mechanisms. The headline-driven and structured news posts are sometimes rewarded by platform algorithms and placed higher in the "trending" or "latest" feeds. However, since the posts of *News Bots* do not necessarily optimize for engagement, their posts may be lost in the deluge of posts.

When *News Bots* contribute to news production and dissemination, they can help audiences stay informed and engaged with the current media environment. For example, during the 2020 coronavirus pandemic, series of automated news accounts promoted good personal health practices, disseminated updates on telemedicine and spread timely information about case numbers and public health measures[257]. Its automation allows for automated and continuous streams of updates, which enhances situational awareness and supports public knowledge during crises.

News Bots can also be deployed to spread false or misleading news. They exploit the credibility associated with news framing while undermining trust in authentic journalism. *News Bots* have been observed to spread false news during political events. For example, in the 2016 US presidential elections, groups of Bots spread low-credibility news sources and polarizing content across social media, amplifying false information on a scale that rivaled mainstream news coverage[258]. Platform algorithms are designed to elevate breaking or high-velocity content, and therefore often surfaces such posts quickly, regardless of source credibility. This algorithmic dynamic blurs the line between legitimate and synthetic journalism, allowing *News Bots* to rival mainstream outlets in their reach while eroding user trust in algorithmic curation itself.

One other type of news these *News Bots* can spread is pink slime news, which are hyper-local news sites that mimic journalism but push partisan or

---

[256] Lokot, Tetyana, and Nicholas Diakopoulos. "News Bots: Automating news and information dissemination on Twitter." *Digital journalism* 4, no. 6 (2016): 682-699.
[257] Al-Rawi, Ahmed, and Vishal Shukla. "Bots as active news promoters: A digital analysis of COVID-19 tweets." *Information* 11, no. 10 (2020): 461.
[258] Shao, Chengcheng, Giovanni Luca Ciampaglia, Onur Varol, Kai-Cheng Yang, Alessandro Flammini, and Filippo Menczer. "The spread of low-credibility content by social bots." *Nature communications* 9, no. 1 (2018): 4787.

sponsored agendas[259]. These outlets have proliferated across the United States, and are often coordinated by parent firms that have political leanings. *News Bots* amplify the content of the root user (i.e., the user that first generates the pink slime news) and give the illusion of grassroots credibility. Further, some *News Bots* can watch for triggers in online conversations like specific words being discussed, and put out a very stylized pink slime story in response to the triggers. These are becoming more possible and common with the use and improvements of LLMs.

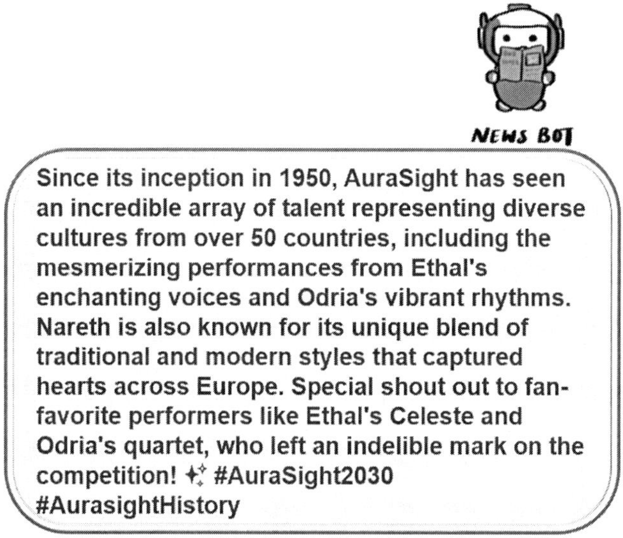

Figure 6.18: Illustration of tweets by a *News Bot* in the AuraSight scenario

Summary. Bot personas characterized by rhetorical strategy are defined by how Bots communicate. **Table 6.2** summarizes the rhetorical strategy and defining User-Content-Interaction pillar of each of the Bot personas we discussed in this subsection. Their influence comes from the discursive and stylistic strategies that they employ, such as their tone, framing, topical focus and use of persuasion cues. Rhetorical personas are most clearly

---

[259] Moore, Ryan, Ross Dahlke, Priyanjana Bengani, and Jeffrey Hancock. "The Consumption of Pink Slime Journalism: Who, What, When, Where, and Why?." (2023). ; Lepird, Christine Sowa, Lynnette Hui Xian Ng, Anna Wu, and Kathleen M. Carley. "What news is shared where and how: A multi-platform analysis of news shared during the 2022 US midterm elections." *Social Media+ Society* 10, no. 2 (2024): 20563051241245950.

characterized by their Content properties, with some also shaped by the User self-presentation (i.e. Self-Declared Bot, News Bot) and Interaction style (i.e. Information Correction Bot).

Persona	Rhetorical Strategy	Defining User-Content-Interaction Pillar	Interaction with Algorithm
Self-Declared Bot	Transparency: opening labeling its automated nature to foster trust and engagement	User: metadata signals (i.e. "bot" in the user name / profile)	Shown by algorithm that it is likely to be a Bot
Announcer Bot	Regularity and authority: framing updates as timely, factual, routine notifications	Content: periodic or trigger-based posts	Exploit algorithmic refresh cycles by maintaining predictable posting cadences
Content Generation Bot	Creativity and novelty: producing original texts, images or media	Content: use of original posts	Amplified through the algorithmic privilege of novelty
Information Correction Bot	Authority and negation: referencing fact-checks and authoritative sources to counter false news	Content: corrective framing Interaction: (sometimes) direct replies	Dependent on the timing, recency and engagement of the information correction
Genre-Specific Bot	Topic consistency: reinforce narratives and identity by focusing exclusively on one theme	Content: majority of posts within one topic frame	Appear as trusted sources of a topic
Conversational Bot	Dialogue: simulating human-like conversations to build rapport and credibility	Content: varied topic frames, higher linguistic complexity	Appear to be socially significant nodes because of their role in sustaining conversations

Persona	Rhetorical Strategy	Defining User-Content-Interaction Pillar	Interaction with Algorithm
Engagement Generation Bot	Emotional salience: using humor and emotional cues to maximize post engagement	Content: affective and stylistic engaging language	Posts incite engagement, thus appearing as organic popularity
News Bot	Journalistic framing: presenting updates as headlines or articles	User: metadata signals (e.g., “news” in user name / profile) Content: headline-style posts	Heavily shaped by algorithmic mechanisms

Figure 6.2: Summary of Bot Personas by Rhetorical Strategy

Usage of Bot Personas

Bot personas are used by different types of social media actors for different purposes. Here are a few examples.

Individual actors are single users that operate alone on social media. Some Bot personas that individuals use are:

1. Amplifier Bots: Individuals use *Amplifier Bots* to boost their personal brands, driving viewership of their content and product.
2. Social Influence Bots: Individuals use *Social Influence Bots* to build community engagement and strengthen digital presence by attracting followers who share aligned interests. These types of Bots can be purchased from underground markets to artificially inflate an individual’s perceived influence[260].

260 Aggarwal, Anupama, and Ponnurangam Kumaraguru. "What they do in shadows: Twitter underground follower market." In *2015 13th Annual Conference on Privacy, Security and Trust (PST)*, pp. 93-100. IEEE, 2015.

3. Cyborgs: Celebrities and activists use *Cyborgs* to assist in periodic and event-based postings[261], in order to maintain an active and authentic online presence.

Organizations are accounts that represent a group of people, such as the government, or a non-profit. The views of the account that are presented in the social media tweets are the views of the organization. Some Bot personas used by organizations include:

1. Announcer Bots: Organizations use *Announcer Bots* to post information updates about its organizations or area of involvement. For example, during the Coronavirus period, vaccination centers used *Announcer Bots* to announce appointment slots for the public to receive their vaccination shots.
2. Chat Bots: Customer service operations often deploy *Chat Bots* for assistance, to respond to Frequently Asked Questions and direct customers to online answers or the appropriate human agent.
3. Information Correction Bots: Fact-checking organizations deploy *Information Correction Bots* to source for and correct false information (i.e., misinformation, disinformation) and sometimes provide the link to the accurate claim.

State-sponsored actors are accounts whose postings are representative and/or directed by the state. Their postings do not represent independent voices but are influenced by state wide or nation-wide political forces. Some types of Bots used by state-sponsored actors include:

1. Amplifier Bot: Governments use *Amplifier Bots* to push out pro-government messages in support of the ruling government party. *Amplifier Bots* are also used during political campaigns to send messages discrediting opposition parties and dissenting citizens.
2. Repeater Bot: States use *Repeater Bots* promote and advertise state agendas and narratives through excessive repeating of the same messages
3. Announcer Bot: Government organizations use *Announcer Bots* to announce key government messages and directives.

---

[261] Ng, Lynnette Hui Xian, Dawn C. Robertson, and Kathleen M. Carley. "Cyborgs for strategic communication on social media." *Big Data & Society* 11, no. 1 (2024): 20539517241231275.

7

DIGITAL INFLUENCE

Influence campaigns can be broadly defined as "coordinated and integrated efforts to accent communications in order to affect attitudes and behaviors"[262]. These campaigns often combine strategic messaging, psychological operations, and targeted dissemination to maximize persuasive impact.

In the online sphere, online influence is not only about what is being talked about, but also about who is talking to whom. For an online information campaign to be successful, the actors need to be shaping both narrative and network of the online space. Bots have been influential in shaping both the narrative and the community, and therefore successful in performing influence operations in online ecosystems.

Operating at scale and at high posting frequency, Bots flood social media with repetitive messages to boost the visibility of selected narratives[263]. When coordinated, Bot networks can rapidly seed and reinforce preferred frames to steer online conversations towards strategic objectives[264]. This

---

262 Larson, Eric V., Richard E. Darilek, Daniel Gibran, Brian Nichiporuk, Amy Richardson, Lowell H. Schwartz, and Cathryn Quantic Thurston. "Foundations of Effective Influence Operations: A Framework for Enhancing Army Capabilities." *Santa Monica, CA: RAND Corporation,* (2009)

263 Chang, Ho-Chun Herbert, Emily Chen, Meiqing Zhang, Goran Muric, and Emilio Ferrara. "Social bots and social media manipulation in 2020: The year in review." In *Handbook of Computational Social Science, Volume 1*, pp. 304-323. Routledge, 2021.; Hajli, Nick, Usman Saeed, Mina Tajvidi, and Farid Shirazi. "Social bots and the spread of disinformation in social media: the challenges of artificial intelligence." *British Journal of Management* 33, no. 3 (2022): 1238-1253.

264 Pacheco, Diogo, Pik-Mai Hui, Christopher Torres-Lugo, Bao Tran Truong, Alessandro Flammini, and Filippo Menczer. "Uncovering coordinated networks on social media: methods and case studies." In *Proceedings of the international AAAI conference on web and social media*, vol. 15, pp. 455-466. 2021.; Hristakieva, Kristina, Stefano Cresci, Giovanni Da San Martino, Mauro Conti, and Preslav

chapter describes how Bots are used in online influence operations and the effect they have on the online discourse.

Mechanisms of Online Influence

A range of complementary frameworks has emerged to characterize online influence – ABC Framework, SCOTCH, DISARM, SAGES, and BEND. Each framework approaches online influence from a different angle. Some focus on who is acting and what they do; others on how campaigns are architected and where they spread, and still others on tactics and techniques that adversaries repeatedly use.

The ABC framework was introduced in 2019 and conceptualizes online disinformation through Actors, Behavior and Content[265]. Actors are manipulative agents with disruptive intent. An example of actors are automated Bot networks. Behaviors describe the tactical repertoire of these actors, such as coordinated amplification, impersonation, or astroturfing. Content refers to the deceptive or polarizing material itself, such as memes, misinformation, fabricated information or miscaptioned images. This model has been expanded to include a D for Distribution, which emphasizes that the algorithmic features of online ecosystems such as recommendation systems and platform-specific affordances, are integral to the reach and impact of the content[266].

The ABC Framework was used by the EU DisinfoLab to analyze the Indian Chronicles campaign. Their analysis uncovered a network of fake media outlets and non-government organizations that discredited Pakistan and promoted Indian interests at the United Nations[267]. The Actors were the users in the Indian Chronicles, many of them were fake personas like an EU

Nakov. "The spread of propaganda by coordinated communities on social media." In *Proceedings of the 14th ACM web science conference 2022*, pp. 191-201. 2022.

[265] François, Camielle (2019). Actors, behaviors, content: A disinformation ABC. *Working Papers from Transatlantic High Level Working Group on Content Moderation Online and Freedom of Expression*

[266] Alaphilippe, Gary M. A. (2020). Adding a 'D'to the ABC disinformation framework. *The Brookings Institute.*

[267] Alaphilippe, Gary M. A, Adamczyk, Roman, and Gregoire, Antoine. Indian Chronicles: Deep Dive into a 15-Year Operation Targeting the EU and UN to Serve Indian Interests. *EU Disinfo Lab* (2020) https://www.disinfo.eu/publications/indian-chronicles-deep-dive-into-a-15-year-operation-targeting-the-eu-and-un-to-serve-indian-interests/

Chronicle journalist. Their behavior included: lobbying members of the EU Parliament through an online honeypot, repackaging and amplifying content, creating and propagating fake media that resonated with the local communities. Their content included: opinion-editorials, fake news websites and social media posts. The distribution mechanism included the use of their fake local media networks and social media platforms.

The key limitation of the ABC framework is its focus on disinformation, but in the real world, there are a lot of other ways to influence others beyond disinformation. Further, the framework is a qualitative framework, which does not give measurable characteristics to interpret the world through the ABC behavior, and it is very much up to the analyst to interpret the event.

The SCOTCH framework was developed with analysts from the US governments, allied governments, and Non-Government Organizations to provide a campaign-level overview of influence operations[268]. The framework summarizes individual influence operations in terms of a campaign overview into Source, Channel, Objective, Target, Composition, and Hook. Source captures the attribution of the campaign, Channel describes the medium of transmission, which are most often social media platforms. Objective denotes the intent of transmission, which can range from undermining trust in elections to promoting geopolitical agendas, and Target specifies the intended audience. The content of a post is separated into Composition and Hook. Composition refers to the types of content deployed, and Hook refers to the persuasive tactics used. The SCOTCH framework has an expanded number of categories than the ABC framework, but still relies on a subjective classification rather than a detailed guidance under each category.

The DISARM framework from the MITRE Corporation stands for Disinformation Analysis & Risk Management, and offers a structured, modular way to analyze influence operations[269]. It does so by categorizing the tactics, techniques and procedures (TTPs) of malicious actors into a Red matrix. This matrix describes offensive maneuvers such as seeding false narratives or orchestrating Bot amplification. There is also a categorization of a complementary Blue matrix, which documents defensive countermeasures like pre-bunking, detection and rapid response interventions. The DISARM

---

[268] Blazek, Sam. SCOTCH: A framework for rapidly assessing influence operations. *GeoTech Cues.* (2021) https://www.atlanticcouncil.org/blogs/geotech-cues/scotch-a-framework-for-rapidly-assessing-influence-operations/

[269] https://www.debunk.org/disarm-framework

framework establishes a common operational vocabulary between the adversary and defender perspective.

The DISARM frame has been used to map how foreign actors leveraged AI-generated content, creation of inauthentic websites, impersonation of legitimate actors and social media disinformation to target vulnerable demographics during the 2024 elections[270]. The DISARM set of maneuvers are presented as a list of micro-level maneuvers that tells the analyst what was performed for influence. The analysts then have to interpret the narratives present. In this case, there are two main types of narratives that were spread: the first type focused on societal vulnerabilities, talking about anti-immigrant narratives, and gender, race, sexual discrimination. The second type aimed to break down the trust in institutions through attacking electoral processes, government agencies and public systems.

The SAGES framework characterized influence through the push of narratives at different stages by adversarial and constructive actors. The stages described in this framework are: Seeding, Amplification, Galvanization, Expansion and Stickiness. This framework was used by the Atlantic Council and the Ministry of Defense, Singapore to profile the narrative influence leading up to the 2021 Myanmar coup and the 2022 Russia-Ukraine conflict [271].

The ABC, SCOTCH and SAGES frameworks are qualitative frameworks on the actions that actors can take for digital influence. The DISARM framework lists what good actors and bad guys can do online. However, these are qualitative frameworks where the interpretation of events can change from analyst to analysts. The BEND framework also looks at actions that actors can perform, but goes beyond these frames to analyze the network of actors.

The BEND framework describes online influence in terms of narrative and community maneuvers. A maneuver is an intentional act carried out by the social media user to achieve a communication goal. These maneuvers are further categorized as affirmative or adverse, which represents the polarity

---

[270] https://www.debunk.org/2024-elections-case-studies-of-foreign-information-manipulation-and-interference-in-eu

[271] Ng, Lynnette Hui Xian, Yukai Zeng, and Muthiah Ponmani. "The Architects of Narrative Evolution: Actor Interventions Across the SAGES Framework in Information Campaigns." *Proceedings of the 59th Haiwaii International Conference on System Sciences.* (2026).

of the influence campaigns. Each BEND maneuver is based on social-psychological theory and empirical evidence. In fact, the DISARM maneuvers can be techniques to implement one of the BEND maneuvers.

Narrative maneuvers use the post content as a means to influence the target audience. Affirmative narrative maneuvers include: Engage, Explain, Excite and Enhance. These maneuvers result in messages that are designed to arouse positive emotions such as joy, excitement or encouragement. Adverse narrative maneuvers include: Dismiss, Distort, Dismay and Distract. These maneuvers incite negative emotions such as sadness or anger. For example, an Excite maneuver might circulate uplifting hashtags to mobilize supporters, while a Dismay maneuver spreads negative framing to dampen enthusiasm.

Community maneuvers target the relational fabric of online groups, seeking either to consolidate or fragment communities around contested narratives. Affirmative maneuvers include: Back, Build, Bridge and Boost. These maneuvers create connections within the network to grow the size of groups. Adverse maneuvers include: Negate, Neutralize, Narrow and Neglect. These maneuvers lead to network communities being broken or dismantled. For example, a Back maneuver might involve Bots coordinating to quote each other's post and provide affirmative words, which serves to boost cross-sharing between communities. A Narrow maneuver could seed divisive hashtags to pit factions of a narrative against each other, resulting in polarized views.

The BEND framework provides a quantitative measurement of the extent and the target of the influence operations, which provides an objective basis of comparison from event to event and actor to actor. This quantitative measurement is operationalized within the ORA-PRO software[272]. This quantitative measurement has been used to track the analysis of online influence in the anti- and pro-vaccination campaign during the initial rollout 2020 coronavirus vaccine[273]. For the pro-vaccine community, the most commonly used maneuver was the Excite maneuver, which was used to encourage others to get the vaccine because of the potential social benefits

---

[272] https://netanomics.com/ora-pro/

[273] Blane, Janice T., Daniele Bellutta, and Kathleen M. Carley. "Social-cyber maneuvers during the COVID-19 vaccine initial rollout: content analysis of tweets." *Journal of Medical Internet Research* 24, no. 3 (2022): e34040.

of lifting nationwide restrictions. The anti-vaccine camp used the Narrow maneuver to discourage people from getting the vaccine.

In this book, the primarily lens for analyzing influence operations is the BEND framework[274], because of its objective measurements and empirical foundations.

Shaping Narratives and Perceptions

Influence in digital spaces is enacted through the orchestration of maneuvers. A series of maneuvers used together creates maneuver sequences. These maneuver sequences make the chosen narratives salient and resonant to the target audience. They can also create an audience for a narrative. Bots shape narratives not only by posting aggressively, but by sequencing influence maneuvers to set the agenda. Bots shape communities not only by interacting with other agents but also by introducing them to each other and supporting leaders and each other's narratives.

We elaborate on a few case studies that use the BEND framework to characterize Bot-driven influence maneuvers. Across political, diplomatic and conflict settings, Bots deploy BEND maneuvers that tilt how issues are framed, emotions are evoked, what groups are present, and who the leaders of the groups are.

In politics, organized and coordinated clusters of Bots push attention by repetitively reinforcing chosen hashtags and narrative tropes[275]. These clusters of Bots also repetitively mention each other, which can build groups or destroy group leaders. They amplify religious political narratives and strengthen the group that supports it using a combination of B's and D's maneuvers, driving polarization within the discourse. They use Back, Build and a little of the Bridge maneuvers to raise allies, and the Distract maneuver to derail adversaries. After the Bot actions, the User x User interaction network becomes polarized. Two echo chambers formed, one around each side of the political discourse: one supporting the government and one opposing the government. Users within each of the groups mostly

---

[274] Carley, Kathleen M. "Social cybersecurity: an emerging science." *Computational and mathematical organization theory* 26, no. 4 (2020): 365-381.

[275] Danaditya, Adya, Lynnette Hui Xian Ng, and Kathleen M. Carley. "From curious hashtags to polarized effect: profiling coordinated actions in Indonesian twitter discourse." *Social Network Analysis and Mining* 12, no. 1 (2022): 105.

interacted with other users in the same group, but rarely interacted with users from the other group.

Figure 8.1 illustrates a polarized network with the AuraSight scenario. This is a User x User interaction network, which means that nodes represent social media users, and User x User links represent an interaction. This figure shows two groups of users highlighted in yellow. These two groups are topical echo chambers. Users from one group mostly interact with users from the same group and seldom interact with users from the other group.

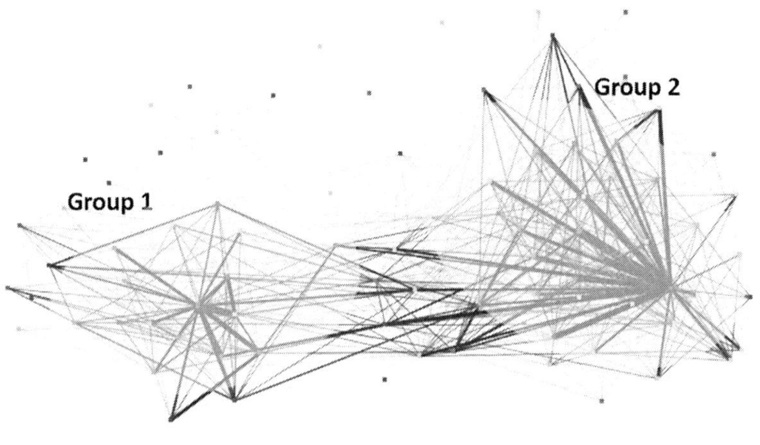

Figure 7.1: Illustration of a polarized network with two topical groups from the AuraSight scenario. Users from one group mostly interact with users from the same group and seldom interact with users from the other group.

In digital warfare, characterizing who holds what stance can help make sense of how maneuvers are being used. Stance is the expression of an opinion towards an entity[276]. This stance can be pro-entity or anti-entity. For example, people that support vaccination would be labeled with a pro-vaccine stance, while people that do not support vaccination would be labeled with an anti-vaccine stance. When there are two groups that are polarized, like **Figure 8.1**, typically one group will have one stance, and another group will have the opposite stance.

[276] Ng, Lynnette Hui Xian, and Kathleen M. Carley. "Is my stance the same as your stance? A cross validation study of stance detection datasets." *Information Processing & Management* 59, no. 6 (2022): 103070.

During the 2022 Russia-Ukraine conflict, pro-Ukraine Bot communities leaned on the B's and E's maneuvers to rally, mobilize and clarify their stance (i.e., pro-Ukraine stance)[277]. These maneuvers are: Back, Build Bridge Boost; and Engage, Excite, Enhance. On the other hand, pro-Russian Bots disproportionately used N's (Negate, Neutralize, Narrow, Neglect) and D's (Dismay, Distract) maneuvers to invalidate opposing voices and inject negative affect. BEND profiles around the hashtags #IstandWithUkraine vs. #IstandWithRussia, and #PutinWarCriminal vs #StopNATO show similar differences in maneuver uses too. During the Kherson counteroffensive, pro-Ukraine streams couple the Excite maneuver with a justice and accountability framing, while pro-Russian streams tried to narrow the topic to recast the conflict as a moral crusade, which was done by intensifying divisive rhetorics laden with historical and nationalistic sentiments (i.e., #ukronazis #natopersists).

Similar patterns of BEND maneuver usage are being echoed in Russian domestic politics. In analysis around the activity of Alexei Navalny, the BEND framework was operationalized to show how Bot-leaning communities favored negative narrative maneuvers (Dismiss, Distort, Distract, Dismay)[278]. The Russian opposition leader Navalny was thought to be poisoned to quell dissent. Anti-opposition Bot tweets focused on undermining Navalny's credibility and blamed the West for staging his poisoning. The negative D' maneuvers were paired with cross-community network actions like Bridge and Boost to shape perceptions around Navalny's death with narratives like: the poisoning was a Western orchestration (Distort/ Distract), delegitimizing Navalny and attacking the credibility of independent media (Dismiss/ Neutralize), and seeding fear and anger to depress support (Dismay).

Outside hot war, digital diplomacy exhibits similar mechanics. In the 2023 dispute between US and China over a Chinese-attributed balloon floating in the US airspace, Bots emphasized community-building B' maneuvers and narrative E' maneuvers. With the B' maneuvers, they exhibited mutual

---

277 Marigliano, Rebecca, Lynnette Hui Xian Ng, and Kathleen M. Carley. "Analyzing digital propaganda and conflict rhetoric: a study on Russia's bot-driven campaigns and counter-narratives during the Ukraine crisis." *Social Network Analysis and Mining* 14, no. 1 (2024): 170.

278 Alieva, Iuliia, J. D. Moffitt, and Kathleen M. Carley. "How disinformation operations against Russian opposition leader Alexei Navalny influence the international audience on Twitter." *Social Network Analysis and Mining* 12, no. 1 (2022): 80.

sharing of messages to prop up the narratives and other accounts. With the E' maneuvers, they used emotional hooks to tug at their countrymen's heartstrings. News Bots are most often Excited and use attention-grabbing headlines, while Bridging Bots most commonly use the Enhance maneuver to keep stories salient and consistent among the clusters.

Overall, Bots use significantly more maneuvers than humans, suggesting that they are designed and primed for influence. There are some types of Bots that use significantly more maneuvers and more specialized maneuvers. Within our Bot typology, Engagement Generation Bots and Social Influence Bots typically use more maneuvers per message. News and Bridging Bots use B's and E's maneuvers to spike salience and capture their audiences[279].

Network structures of Bots and humans also affect the type of maneuvers used. Bots have more star-like patterns, which are well-suited for maneuvers like Back and Boost that enables message broadcast and agent support[280]. Humans have a more hierarchal interaction graph patterns, which favors multi-hop conversational cascades, and settings where Explain/Engage maneuvers tend to carry farther[281].

Influence maneuvers shape perceptions by playing on human cognitive biases (which we will talk more about in the next chapter, Chapter 8). Maneuvers like Back, Boost and Distract exploit the Illusory Truth Effect to saturate social media feeds with familiar cues, in hopes that these repeated claims will translate into beliefs[282]. Maneuvers like Excite and Dismay play on the Affect Bias by evoking emotions to shortcut deliberation. Emotionally arousing content travels farther so these maneuvers leverage the virality gradient to accelerate their narrative spread[283]. Maneuvers like

---

[279] Ng, Lynnette Hui Xian, and Kathleen M. Carley. "Deflating the Chinese balloon: types of Twitter bots in US-China balloon incident." *EPJ Data Science* 12, no. 1 (2023): 63.

[280] Ng, Lynnette Hui Xian, and Kathleen M. Carley. "A global comparison of social media bot and human characteristics." *Scientific Reports* 15, no. 1 (2025): 10973.

[281] Beskow, David M., and Kathleen M. Carley. "Agent based simulation of bot disinformation maneuvers in Twitter." In *2019 Winter simulation conference (WSC)*, pp. 750-761. IEEE, 2019.

[282] Udry, Jessica, and Sarah J. Barber. "The illusory truth effect: A review of how repetition increases belief in misinformation." *Current Opinion in Psychology* 56 (2024): 101736.

[283] Rathje, Steve, and Jay J. Van Bavel. "The psychology of virality." *Trends in Cognitive Sciences* (2025). ; Berger, Jonah, and Katherine L. Milkman. "What

Back/Build, Excite/Engage makes certain issues hyper-visible through the use of the Availability Bias. These maneuvers make the narratives more visible through repetition and engagement, and narratives that are more available are perceived to be more believable. Excite/Enhance maneuvers increase the coherency of the narrative and provide the illusion of exploratory depth. Enhance increases the coherency of an explanation. An explanation that is more coherent is more believable. The more believable the topic, the more the narrative will be talked about[284]. These influence maneuvers shift what the public thinks about the topic, and triggers feelings about the same topic. When used excessively by Bots, this creates a perception pipeline from attention to affect to apparent consensus. This pipeline is effective because it is a cognitive path that beliefs harden and behaviors follow[285].

---

makes online content viral?." *Journal of marketing research* 49, no. 2 (2012): 192-205.

[284] Reber, Rolf, Norbert Schwarz, and Piotr Winkielman. "Processing fluency and aesthetic pleasure: Is beauty in the perceiver's processing experience?." *Personality and social psychology review* 8, no. 4 (2004): 364-382. ; Currie, Gregory, and Jon Jureidini. "Narrative and coherence." *Mind & language* 19, no. 4 (2004): 409-427.

[285] Bandura, Albert, Nancy E. Adams, and Janice Beyer. "Cognitive processes mediating behavioral change." *Journal of personality and social psychology* 35, no. 3 (1977): 125.

8

HUMAN BIASES

In the digital sphere, human attention is a scarce resource, so individuals rely on mental shortcuts to cope with the overwhelming volume of information that is being created and pushed to their feeds in real-time. These mental shortcuts are also termed as social cognition, which are heuristics that our mind uses to make sense of the overwhelming amount of information. When making decisions about information (i.e., what to believe, what is false), people can be biased in processing data, because of the environment or their past experiences. This process is known as **cognitive biases**, which are systematic patterns of deviation from normative judgment[286]. These biases help us humans decide what to focus our attention towards and what to ignore, helping us to find meaning through the noise, especially in digital environments where stimuli are abundant.

Bots exploit the psychological regularities of social cognition and cognitive biases by tailoring their message framing and the repetition of messages to align with human heuristics. In doing so, they transform these individual vulnerabilities into scalable tools of persuasion.

This chapter reviews core cognitive biases that constrain decision making in the online social media ecosystems, then analyzes how Bot strategies systematically exploit these biases to shape online discourse and behavior.

Cognitive Biases and Decision Making

Cognitive biases are systematic departures from rational judgments. Such departures emerge because humans rely on heuristics to filter and respond to the overwhelming capacity and complexity of information. In the social media ecosystem, these biases are exploited by social media actors to direct the audience's attention in the attention-scarce environment. Understanding

---

[286] Tversky, Amos, and Daniel Kahneman. "Judgment under Uncertainty: Heuristics and Biases: Biases in judgments reveal some heuristics of thinking under uncertainty." *science* 185, no. 4157 (1974): 1124-1131.

how these biases operate, and how they can be leveraged is important for mapping the mechanics of online influence.

Judgment heuristics. There are three foundational heuristics that humans employ when evaluating uncertain information[287]. These heuristics are: judgment by representativeness, judgment by availability, and judgment by anchoring. Judgment by representativeness occurs when people judge the credibility of a message based on whether it looks like a familiar prototype. For example, people are more likely to believe a Bot if it writes like a human[288]. Judgment by availability occurs when the perceived likelihood of an event is influenced by the ease with which the relevant information can be retrieved or assessed. For example, if a piece of news "kimchi can cure the flu" is repeated incessantly by all the Korean women one encounters, one is more likely to believe this remedy. Judgment by anchoring occurs when prior anchors influence the evaluation of an outcome. These prior anchors could be past personal experience or existing beliefs. If someone had a relative who had the flu, ate kimchi regularly and recovered from the flu, one is more likely to believe in the power of kimchi from curing the flu.

Each one of these heuristics is associated with a particular set of cognitive bias. Here, we look at eight common biases that occur in social media. Judgment by Representativeness is associated with homophily bias and authority bias. Judgment by Availability is associated with affect bias, negativity bias, illusory truth effect and availability bias. Judgment by anchoring is associated with cognitive dissonance and confirmation bias.

Homophily bias is the tendency to favor information from people perceived as similar in identity or worldview to oneself. This bias is associated with the judgment by representativeness heuristic, because it describes how people favor information that are representative of how they view themselves and the identities they affiliate themselves with. Identities are usually self-presented in a user's profile. For example, if the user writes in his profile that he is a "dad", we can assume that he identifies strongly with family narratives. Both on social media and in real-life, people with the same sets of interests and identities are more likely to be friends and

---

[287] Tversky, Amos, and Daniel Kahneman. "Judgment under Uncertainty: Heuristics and Biases: Biases in judgments reveal some heuristics of thinking under uncertainty." *science* 185, no. 4157 (1974): 1124-1131.

[288] Kenny, Ryan, Baruch Fischhoff, Alex Davis, Kathleen M. Carley, and Casey Canfield. "Duped by bots: why some are better than others at detecting fake social media personas." *Human factors* 66, no. 1 (2024): 88-102.

converse about similar topics[289]. (We talked about social identities and affiliations in Chapter 5.)

Social media strongly amplifies the homophily bias, with many observations on how users cluster into groups that are homogeneous ideologically or identity-wise. Such groups are sometimes termed as echo-chambers, because they reinforce group consensus by echoing each other, and filter out external perspectives[290]. One example of homophilic alignment is when people align their actions and messages with others whose metadata contain the same set of identities[291]. This homophily bias greatly affects information diffusion on social media. People that share the same location or activity patterns are 15-25% more likely to interact with each other, which therefore creates effective information conduits[292].

Availability bias is when narratives are more believable because of their increased repetition. Availability bias is heightened in digital environments by algorithmic ranking and repetition, which can make certain narratives feel omnipresent regardless of their objective frequency. Repetition is typically done through the sharing post mechanism, because posts with more engagement are amplified algorithmically. This bias is associated with the judgment by availability heuristic because it describes the increased believability of the narrative when the narrative is more available.

During the 2020 coronavirus pandemic, the repeated anti-vaccination posts created the impression that hesitancy was the dominant sentiment, despite mixed survey data about vaccination[293]. A survey in 2024 showed that the

---

[289] Aiello, Luca Maria, Alain Barrat, Rossano Schifanella, Ciro Cattuto, Benjamin Markines, and Filippo Menczer. "Friendship prediction and homophily in social media." *ACM Transactions on the Web (TWEB)* 6, no. 2 (2012): 1-33.

[290] Mahmoudi, Amin, Dariusz Jemielniak, and Leon Ciechanowski. "Echo chambers in online social networks: A systematic literature review." *IEEE Access* 12 (2024): 9594-9620.

[291] Hakobyan, Zaruhi, and Christos Koulovatianos. "Populism and Polarization in Social Media Without Fake News: The Vicious Circle of Biases, Beliefs and Network Homophily." *Higher School of Economics Research Paper No. WP BRP* 227 (2020).

[292] De Choudhury, Munmun, Hari Sundaram, Ajita John, Doree Duncan Seligmann, and Aisling Kelliher. "" Birds of a Feather": Does User Homophily Impact Information Diffusion in Social Media?." *arXiv preprint arXiv:1006.1702* (2010).

[293] Honcharov, Vlad, Jiawei Li, Maribel Sierra, Natalie A. Rivadeneira, Kristan Olazo, Thu T. Nguyen, Tim K. Mackey, and Urmimala Sarkar. "Public figure vaccination rhetoric and vaccine hesitancy: retrospective Twitter analysis." *JMIR*

huge media and social media attention on breast cancer results in women having heightened fear of having breast cancer as compared to other chronic conditions[294]. Such perceptions lead to a narrow scope of information-seeking and health preventing behaviors from women, as they tend to focus more on cancer prevention rather than their overall health.

Availability bias can be triggered by influential users because the algorithm props up the visibility of these users. A message that is shared by influencer accounts that have a high number of followers is typically retweeted more times than the average user's post, and is judged by both the platform recommendation algorithm and other users as being more representative of reality.

Illusory Truth Effect occurs when repetition of sets of phrases alone increases the perceived accuracy of information. This bias is associated with the judgment by availability heuristic, because of the availability of repeated phrases. On social media platforms, slogans like "vaccines cause infertility" can increase the number of people who believe the message simply through sheer frequency of exposure. Illusory truth effect differs from availability bias in the manner by which the information is repeated[295]. Availability bias makes use of the platform's algorithm for repeated exposure through mechanisms like retweets, while illusory truth effect occurs when encountering the same claim multiple times makes it seem more accurate. In short, Availability bias is the repetition of the exact same message, while Illusory Truth Effect is repeated phrases.

In the 2020 coronavirus context, survey participants that saw anti-vaccination headlines at least twice rated them more accurate than those who saw them only once, demonstrating how perceived information accuracy changes with repeated exposure of the exact same phrasing of information[296]. The repeated information is often perceived to be more

---

infodemiology 3, no. 1 (2023): e40575. ; Sallam, Malik. "COVID-19 vaccine hesitancy worldwide: a concise systematic review of vaccine acceptance rates." *Vaccines* 9, no. 2 (2021): 160.

[294] Aguirre-Camacho, Aldo, Helena Gandía-Abellán, and Judit Tirado-Muñoz. ""I Think I Do but I Don't": Heightened (Breast) Cancer Concern as a Function of Availability Bias." *Women* 4, no. 2 (2024): 201-215.

[295] Ng, Lynnette Hui Xian, Wenqi Zhou, and Kathleen M. Carley. "Exploring cognitive bias triggers in covid-19 misinformation tweets: A bot vs. human perspective." *arXiv preprint arXiv:2406.07293* (2024).

[296] de Saint Laurent, Constance, Gillian Murphy, Karen Hegarty, and Ciara M. Greene. "Measuring the effects of misinformation exposure and beliefs on

truthful than new information; in fact, one only needs two repeats to trigger the cognitive bias[297].

Cognitive Dissonance arises when individuals encounter information that contradicts their beliefs. This contradiction produces psychological discomfort, which can either cause the individual to agree with the information or dismiss the information. This bias is associated with the judgment by anchoring heuristic because the individual anchors the new information with his current beliefs, and after which, finds that the new information contradicts the current beliefs.

An example of the cognitive dissonance in play is when fact-checking interventions are frequently rejected by conspiracy theorists or partisans to maintain congruence with their world beliefs and political identities[298]. Users can also decide to change their stance to blend into the prevailing conversation and community. Across 2020-2021, about 1% of the users on X changed their stances about the coronavirus vaccination to fit into their discussion threads[299]. Algorithms exacerbate cognitive dissonance by enabling selective exposure, allowing users to avoid dissonance altogether by curating feeds that reinforce pre-existing views, which are inferred by the messages the users like or the people they follow[300].

Confirmation Bias is the tendency to seek and interpret evidence to be consistent with prior beliefs. This bias is associated with the judgment by anchoring heuristic, where the audience's perception is anchored to their prior belief about the topic. This bias is reinforced by social media

---

behavioural intentions: a COVID-19 vaccination study." *Cognitive Research: Principles and Implications* 7, no. 1 (2022): 87.

[297] Hassan, Aumyo, and Sarah J. Barber. "The effects of repetition frequency on the illusory truth effect." *Cognitive research: principles and implications* 6, no. 1 (2021): 38.

[298] Walter, Nathan, Jonathan Cohen, R. Lance Holbert, and Yasmin Morag. "Fact-checking: A meta-analysis of what works and for whom." *Political communication* 37, no. 3 (2020): 350-375. ; Pretus, Clara, Camila Servin-Barthet, Elizabeth A. Harris, William J. Brady, Oscar Vilarroya, and Jay J. Van Bavel. "The role of political devotion in sharing partisan misinformation and resistance to fact-checking." *Journal of Experimental Psychology: General* 152, no. 11 (2023): 3116.

[299] Ng, Lynnette Hui Xian, and Kathleen M. Carley. "Pro or anti? a social influence model of online stance flipping." *IEEE Transactions on Network Science and Engineering* 10, no. 1 (2022): 3-19.

[300] Wamsley, Dené EM. *Algorithms vs. Human Nature: A Tale of Selective Exposure*. University of Arkansas, 2022.

algorithms, which deliver more of what the users already endorse through analyzing their content engagement habits, and creating self-reinforcing feedback loops. This process further narrows the range of perspectives that users encounter, locking individuals further into topically and ideologically consistent environments[301]. Studies of the Facebook and X platforms show that misinformation persists because users preferentially interact with content that validates their worldview, while ignoring and discounting corrective information[302]. During health pandemics, confirmation bias fuels opinion polarization and improved satisfaction of users as users interacted more with narratives that resonated with their anxieties and prior beliefs[303].

Affect bias reflects how emotions shape judgment. When triggered, individuals rely on their feelings rather than accuracy cues to evaluate information. This bias is associated with the judgment by availability heuristic because the emotions associated with the narratives make them more memorable, and therefore more accessible, or available to be recalled. On social media, emotionally charged content spreads more rapidly than neutral information[304]. This is especially so when the emotions contain fear[305], outrage, anger[306], or incite emotions with moralized content[307]. For example, studies of activity on X during the 2020 coronavirus pandemic

---

[301] Spohr, Dominic. "Fake news and ideological polarization: Filter bubbles and selective exposure on social media." *Business information review* 34, no. 3 (2017): 150-160.

[302] Lewandowsky, Stephan, Ullrich KH Ecker, Colleen M. Seifert, Norbert Schwarz, and John Cook. "Misinformation and its correction: Continued influence and successful debiasing." *Psychological science in the public interest* 13, no. 3 (2012): 106-131. ; Schulz, Peter J., and Kent Nakamoto. *Worse Than Ignorance: The Challenge of Health Misinformation*. Cambridge University Press, 2024.

[303] Li, Teng, and Wander Jager. "How availability heuristic, confirmation bias and fear may drive societal polarisation: an opinion dynamics simulation of the case of COVID-19 vaccination." *Journal of Artificial Societies and Social Simulation* 26, no. 4 (2023): 2.

[304] Berger, J., & Milkman, K. (2010). Social transmission, emotion, and the virality of online content. *Wharton research paper*, *106*, 1-52.

[305] Horner, Christy Galletta, Dennis Galletta, Jennifer Crawford, and Abhijeet Shirsat. "Emotions: The unexplored fuel of fake news on social media." In *Fake news on the internet*, pp. 147-174. Routledge, 2023.

[306] Wollebæk, Dag, Rune Karlsen, Kari Steen-Johnsen, and Bernard Enjolras. "Anger, fear, and echo chambers: The emotional basis for online behavior." *Social Media+ Society* 5, no. 2 (2019): 2056305119829859.

[307] Brady, William J., Julian A. Wills, John T. Jost, Joshua A. Tucker, and Jay J. Van Bavel. "Emotion shapes the diffusion of moralized content in social networks." *Proceedings of the National Academy of Sciences* 114, no. 28 (2017): 7313-7318.

found that posts framing vaccines in terms of fear or moral violation (i.e., claims that governments were hiding the truth or pharmaceutical companies were gunning for profits), were shared and engaged with at a much higher rate than neutral health updates[308].

Negativity bias is a subset of Affect Bias. Social media users attend more to negative than positive information, and negative posts receive more engagement on social media platforms. This bias is associated with the judgment by availability heuristic, because the negative emotions associated with the information makes the narratives more memorable and accessible to be discussed or disputed.

Analysis of news engagement across multiple platforms show that regardless of topic, posts emphasizing conflict, loss or outrage attract significantly higher user interaction rates than positive or neutral posts[309]. Recent studies demonstrate that while fact-checking efforts can slow the spread of false information, they are often framed in negative terms, which reduces their effectiveness and can even bring the user's attention to the false information itself, allowing the original false information to spread farther and faster than factual corrections[310].

These biases illustrate why social media can be a powerful environment for influence campaigns. At any point in time, the user receives a lot of information on social media. A person's typical attention span for a piece of information on social media is just 47 seconds[311], which means that content creators have to attract attention for people to remember their content. Cognitive biases allow humans to perform effective judgment on which content to interact with, but these very shortcuts can become leverage

---

[308] Marttila, Eetu, and Aki Koivula. "Framing, emotions, and morality: Understanding media influence on moral attitudes towards the unvaccinated during COVID-19." *The Social Science Journal* 62, no. 2 (2025): 478-493.

[309] Aldous, Kholoud Khalil, Jisun An, and Bernard J. Jansen. "What really matters?: characterising and predicting user engagement of news postings using multiple platforms, sentiments and topics." *Behaviour & Information Technology* 42, no. 5 (2023): 545-568.

[310] King, Kelvin K., and Diego Escobari. "Can Correction Messages Reduce the Spread of Fake News on Social Media? The Impact of Information Updates on the Effectiveness of Corrections." *Journal of Management Information Systems* 42, no. 3 (2025): 706-736.

[311] Mark, Gloria. *Attention span: A groundbreaking way to restore balance, happiness and productivity*. Harlequin, 2023.

points for manipulation. Recognizing these mechanisms is central to understanding and predicting potentially viral content.

Bot Strategies and Bias Exploitation

Bots transform individual human cognitive vulnerabilities into scalable strategies of persuasion, turning biases into predictable shifts in attention, emotion and perceived consensus. For example, in conflict storytelling, coordinated Bot communities time and frame messages to moralize allies and delegitimize adversaries, making their chosen narratives feel salient, urgent and socially validated[312]. Here, we elaborate on the strategies that Bots use to exploit each of the cognitive biases. These strategies can also be implemented through the BEND information maneuver framework that aims to influence audiences through narrative manipulation and network community maneuvers[313]. The BEND framework has 16 maneuvers, four for each letter, and is described in detail in Chapter 8.

Homophily Bias. Bots exploit homophily bias by preferentially attaching to like-minded accounts and themes, creating self-affirming feedback loops that strengthen the community identity. Experiments and large scale observations show that Bots actively seek to interact with others with similar political ideologies[314]. As Bots introduce people that express similar ideologies online to each other, they grow the groups, which increases the occurrence and presence of ideologies in people's feed, leading to ideologically skewed feeds and reinforcing partisan echo chambers[315]. Even modern AI conversational Bots that are created using Large Language Models (LLM) like OpenAI's ChatGPT and Anthropic's Claude exhibit the same homophily bias tendency in synthetic societies. In a simulated

---

[312] Marigliano, Rebecca, Lynnette Hui Xian Ng, and Kathleen M. Carley. "Analyzing digital propaganda and conflict rhetoric: a study on Russia's bot-driven campaigns and counter-narratives during the Ukraine crisis." *Social Network Analysis and Mining* 14, no. 1 (2024): 170.

[313] Carley, Kathleen M. "Social cybersecurity: an emerging science." *Computational and mathematical organization theory* 26, no. 4 (2020): 365-381.

[314] Chen, Wen, Diogo Pacheco, Kai-Cheng Yang, and Filippo Menczer. "Neutral bots probe political bias on social media." *Nature communications* 12, no. 1 (2021): 5580.

[315] Hicks, Matthew, and M. Kathleen. "BEND Battle: An Agent Based Simulation of Social-Cyber Maneuvers." International Conference on Social Computing, Behavioral-Cultural Modeling & Prediction and Behavior Representation in Modeling and Simulation. Working Papers (2023).

community of more than 33,000 such LLM-powered Bots, communities emerge around Bots that post similar content, and in similar languages[316]. Homophily bias also increases influence. When the other user "looks like me", the message acceptance and spread increase, especially so for identity-relevant narratives (i.e., partisan, demographic)[317].

Within propaganda and protest campaigns, Bot networks often display homophily bias at scale. They amplify one another more than they engage with other humans, and this gathering of similar Bots make them more influential[318] as they congregate in star networks and occupy central positions in the network. When pro- or anti-war clusters form around recurring slogans and symbols, homophily concentrates attention and primes audiences to accept in-group conflict stories as common sense[319].

Availability Bias. People judge importance by what is most visible and easiest to recall. Bots convert this cognitive shortcut into a persuasive strategy by pushing bursts of narratives into a story's life cycle[320] and targeting high-follower and influential accounts via replies and mentions[321]. Such strategies leverage algorithms to increase the visibility of a narrative through creating high engagement of posts or creating very recent posts.

---

[316] He, James K., Felix PS Wallis, Andrés Gvirtz, and Steve Rathje. "Artificial intelligence chatbots mimic human collective behaviour." *British Journal of Psychology* (2024).

[317] Shang, Yingdan, Bin Zhou, Xiang Zeng, Ye Wang, Han Yu, and Zhong Zhang. "Predicting the popularity of online content by modeling the social influence and homophily features." *Frontiers in Physics* 10 (2022): 915756. ; Taylor, Cameron E., Alexander V. Mantzaris, and Ivan Garibay. "Exploring how homophily and accessibility can facilitate polarization in social networks." *Information* 9, no. 12 (2018): 325.

[318] Williams, Evan M., Valerie Novak, Dylan Blackwell, Paul Platzman, Ian McCulloh, and Nolan Edward Phillips. "Homophily and transitivity in bot disinformation networks." In *2020 Seventh International Conference on Social Networks Analysis, Management and Security (SNAMS)*, pp. 1-7. IEEE, 2020.

[319] Moghaddam, Samaneh Hosseini, Mandana Khademi, and Maghsoud Abbaspour. "Does homophily make socialbots more influential? Exploring infiltration strategies." *arXiv preprint arXiv:1903.06827* (2019).

[320] Ferrara, Emilio. "Measuring social spam and the effect of bots on information diffusion in social media." In *Complex spreading phenomena in social systems: Influence and contagion in real-world social networks*, pp. 229-255. Cham: Springer International Publishing, 2018.

[321] Kim, Seungbae, and Jinyoung Han. "Detecting engagement bots on social influencer marketing." In International Conference on Social Informatics, pp. 124-136. Cham: Springer International Publishing, 2020.

The social media platform recommendation algorithms typically promote the most recent posts and posts with high engagement[322]. Using the availability bias triggers with the social media platforms' algorithms creates a "flood-the-zone" effect[323], which floods audiences' social media feeds with their desired narratives, so that the audience constantly sees the same narratives.

In practice, availability bias tactics could manifest in coordinated hashtags or URL pushes, which can saturate social media feeds in and set the agenda, bring attention to the narratives[324]. Within the BEND influence maneuver framework, possible maneuvers to leverage the availability bias heuristic would be the Back/Build/Boost maneuver to raise visibility of a message or a person, or the Negate/Neutralize/Dismiss maneuver to discredit competing frames and therefore reduce the visibility of those frames.

Cognitive Dissonance is the tension between the audience and their internal beliefs because of the contraction of information. Bot campaigns can leverage on the cognitive dissonance by delegitimizing corrections of fake news. They frame the corrections as biased, foreign or irrelevant, so audiences can restore coherence without updating their belief in the fake information[325]. This reduces the dissonance between the audience and the contradictory information, which implicitly helps the audience who would be going increasingly tense from the dis-harmony of information, to ignore the correction. The audience thus maintains their belief in the incorrect information, removing dissonance.

Bots can rapidly resolve their own cognitive dissonance with their social network by changing their stance towards an entity to match the other users

---

322 Gillespie, Tarleton. "# trendingistrending: When algorithms become culture." In *Algorithmic cultures*, pp. 64-87. Routledge, 2016.

323 Maréchal, Nathalie. "Automation, algorithms, and politics| when bots tweet: Toward a normative framework for bots on social networking sites (feature)." International Journal of Communication 10 (2016): 10.

324 Ciampaglia, Giovanni Luca, Azadeh Nematzadeh, Filippo Menczer, and Alessandro Flammini. "How algorithmic popularity bias hinders or promotes quality." *Scientific reports* 8, no. 1 (2018): 15951.

325 Wang, Rui, Yuan He, Jing Xu, and Hongzhong Zhang. "Fake news or bad news? Toward an emotion-driven cognitive dissonance model of misinformation diffusion." Asian Journal of Communication 30, no. 5 (2020): 317-342.

that they are interacting with[326]. Further, a group of coordinating Bots can pressure a target user to resolve his cognitive dissonance by changing their stance towards their stance, thus winning the user over to their side. Tightly connected crowds can amplify dysfunctional thinking and cascade the dissonance to spread a desired narrative from small communities to society-wide uptake[327].

This cognitive dissonance can also be used for prosocial means. Conversational Bots can gently surface gaps between a user's stated values and portrayed behavior, soothe them over with extensive elaborations, and increase the user's intention to comply with public-health guidance[328]. Such studies demonstrate that interventions can use the cognitive dissonance trigger to steer people toward more accurate information.

Within the BEND maneuvers, the Explain/Enhance maneuvers provide rationales to ease the tension between the reader's belief and the narrative presented. The Back/Build/Boost maneuvers surround users with supportive signals towards the "right" position (often the position desired by the Bot networks). The Negate/Neutralize/Dismiss maneuvers offer reasons to exit the dissonance by discrediting the messengers.

Confirmation Bias. People preferentially seek, notice and share information that aligns with their prior beliefs. On social media platforms, this bias is amplified by the people and trends they follow, which affects what the algorithm shows them. Bots fit neatly into this by feeding congenial links and slogans to like-minded users and pushing one-sided frames that match existing views of the users[329]. These users are highly likely to adopt the frames presented to them because they are consistent with their inner beliefs. Such actions create polarized stances as users constantly read information from only one particular point of view. At the ecosystem level, researchers argue that cognitive biases like confirmation bias make

---

[326] Ng, Lynnette Hui Xian, and Kathleen M. Carley. "Pro or anti? a social influence model of online stance flipping." IEEE Transactions on Network Science and Engineering 10, no. 1 (2022): 3-19.

[327] Seeme, Fatima, David Green, and Carlo Kopp. "Ignorance of the crowd: dysfunctional thinking in social networks." Frontiers in Communication 10 (2025): 1547489.

[328] Kim, WooJin, and Yuhosua Ryoo. "Hypocrisy induction: Using chatbots to promote COVID-19 social distancing." Cyberpsychology, Behavior, and Social Networking 25, no. 1 (2022): 27-36.

[329] Aldayel, Abeer, and Walid Magdy. "Characterizing the role of bots' in polarized stance on social media." Social Network Analysis and Mining 12, no. 1 (2022): 30.

the public especially vulnerable to both intentional and accidental misinformation, which Bots exploit by amplifying agreeable claims and filtering out the non-conforming ones[330].

Experiments show that Bots can amplify perceptual biases. After interacting with content from social media Bots, people overestimate the prevalence of Bots, are more susceptible to conflicting information, and tighten their confirmation bias loop around their prior beliefs[331].

Within the BEND repertoire, confirmation bias is leveraged through the Back/Build/Boost maneuvers to surround users with in-group signals and narratives. Engage/Enhance maneuvers reinforce interpretations that are consistent with the existing schema. Negate/Dismiss maneuvers strip credibility from dis-confirming sources. Bots employ these influence maneuvers to collectively steer selective exposure and belief persistence. Design work on biased Bots also maps how confirmation bias can be used as a counter-strategy. By studying reactions and perceptions of users exposed to counter-evidence in controlled dialog settings, Conversational Bots that present structured opposing arguments can be used to break the cycle of confirmation bias[332].

Illusory Truth Effect. Direct repetition makes statements feel more true, because repeated claims are easier to process, and subsequently are perceived to be more truthful than new statements[333]. A single prior exposure can raise the perception of truth judgments of a later encounter of the exact same fake-news headlines, and this effect persists over time[334].

---

330 Ciampaglia, Giovanni L., and Filippo Menczer. "Misinformation and biases infect social media, both intentionally and accidentally." The Conversation 20, no. 1 (2018): 1-4.

331 Yan, Harry Yaojun, Kai-Cheng Yang, James Shanahan, and Filippo Menczer. "Exposure to social bots amplifies perceptual biases and regulation propensity." Scientific Reports 13, no. 1 (2023): 20707.

332 Dingler, Tilman, Ashris Choudhury, and Vassilis Kostakos. "Biased bots: Conversational agents to overcome polarization." In Proceedings of the 2018 ACM international joint conference and 2018 international symposium on pervasive and ubiquitous computing and wearable computers, pp. 1664-1668. 2018.

333 Fazio, Lisa K., Nadia M. Brashier, B. Keith Payne, and Elizabeth J. Marsh. "Knowledge does not protect against illusory truth." *Journal of experimental psychology: general* 144, no. 5 (2015): 993.

334 Pennycook, Gordon, Tyrone D. Cannon, and David G. Rand. "Prior exposure increases perceived accuracy of fake news." *Journal of experimental psychology: general* 147, no. 12 (2018): 1865.

Bots make use of this strategy by saturating the social media platforms with near-duplicate headlines, templated memes, and quote-tweet storms, ensuring that the audiences encounter the same claim multiple times before their mental deliberation catches up[335].

During the 2020 coronavirus pandemic, Russian Bots injected thousands of posts on both pro- and anti-vaccine angles, sustaining the same talking points over months. This continuous discussion manufactured the perception that the issue of vaccination was highly salient, and the issue perpetually visible to the recommendation algorithms and audience's feeds[336]. False news like "coronavirus is an engineered virus" were shared often on social media because people are more likely to share information that they have repeatedly encountered[337].

Within the BEND repertoire, the Back/ Build/ Boost maneuvers drive the repeated exposures of these maneuvers and so powers the Illusory Truth Effect. The Distract maneuver can reduce the Illusory Truth Effect because the maneuver can be used to repeatedly inject alternative talking points to block out competing claims.

Affect / Negativity Bias. Emotionally charged content spreads faster and farther. False rumors go viral when they carry more positive sentiment and words tied to trust, anticipation and anger. In fact, false rumors that have above average (more than 1 standard deviation) positive sentiment have a 37% longer lifespan and reaches 61% more users[338]. Bots lean into that by injecting moral and emotional language at scale for their bursts of messages

---

335 Pennycook, Gordon, Tyrone D. Cannon, and David G. Rand. "Prior exposure increases perceived accuracy of fake news." *Journal of experimental psychology: general* 147, no. 12 (2018): 1865. ; Danaditya, Adya, Lynnette Hui Xian Ng, and Kathleen M. Carley. "From curious hashtags to polarized effect: profiling coordinated actions in indonesian twitter discourse." *Social Network Analysis and Mining* 12, no. 1 (2022): 105.

336 Broniatowski, David A., Amelia M. Jamison, SiHua Qi, Lulwah AlKulaib, Tao Chen, Adrian Benton, Sandra C. Quinn, and Mark Dredze. "Weaponized health communication: Twitter bots and Russian trolls amplify the vaccine debate." *American journal of public health* 108, no. 10 (2018): 1378-1384.

337 Hassan, Aumyo, and Sarah J. Barber. "The effects of repetition frequency on the illusory truth effect." *Cognitive research: principles and implications* 6, no. 1 (2021): 38.

338 Pröllochs, Nicolas, Dominik Bär, and Stefan Feuerriegel. "Emotions explain differences in the diffusion of true vs. false social media rumors." *Scientific Reports* 11, no. 1 (2021): 22721.

and headlines, to make people feel before they deliberate[339]. Emotional language through affective words is recognized more quickly and accurately than neutral ones, which makes Bot-authored emotion-packed posts easier to notice, process and remember[340]. Observations of brand and news chatter show that emotions and volume of messages are primary tools that Bots use to drive manipulation. Analyses of the 2020 coronavirus pandemic era[341] and 2021 Indian-Pakistan conflict[342] find that Bots were disproportionately tweeting and retweeting about stress and fear to arouse human fear. Emotions also heighten the effect of cognitive dissonance. When information is wrapped in emotions like anger, anxiety or hope, readers often resolve the dissonance through sharing and endorsement rather than scrutiny[343]. This process helps false narratives diffuse under stress.

Negative emotion is especially salient online because negative material is prioritized in attention and memory, and this regularity is called the negativity bias[344]. People remember the negative stories more, and therefore these stories are more likely to be shared. Bots magnify negativity bias by pushing inflammatory and negative narratives to influential humans, which can therefore exacerbate conflict[345]. For narratives examined in over 172,000 tweets of health discussions, Bots were more negative than

---

[339] Liu, Xia. "A big data approach to examining social bots on Twitter." *Journal of Services Marketing* 33, no. 4 (2019): 369-379.

[340] Kousta, Stavroula-Thaleia, David P. Vinson, and Gabriella Vigliocco. "Emotion words, regardless of polarity, have a processing advantage over neutral words." *Cognition* 112, no. 3 (2009): 473-481.

[341] Elayan, Suzanne, and Martin Sykora. "Digital intermediaries in pandemic times: social media and the role of bots in communicating emotions and stress about Coronavirus." *Journal of Computational Social Science* 7, no. 3 (2024): 2481-2504.

[342] Ng, Lynnette Hui Xian, and Kathleen M. Carley. "Bot-based emotion behavior differences in images during Kashmir black day event." In International Conference on Social Computing, Behavioral-Cultural Modeling and Prediction and Behavior Representation in Modeling and Simulation, pp. 184-194. Cham: Springer International Publishing, 2021.

[343] Taddicken, Monika, and Laura Wolff. "'Fake News' in science communication: emotions and strategies of coping with dissonance online." *Media and Communication* 8, no. 1 (2020): 206-217.

[344] Rozin, Paul, and Edward B. Royzman. "Negativity bias, negativity dominance, and contagion." *Personality and social psychology review* 5, no. 4 (2001): 296-320.

[345] Stella, Massimo, Emilio Ferrara, and Manlio De Domenico. "Bots increase exposure to negative and inflammatory content in online social systems." Proceedings of the National Academy of Sciences 115, no. 49 (2018): 12435-12440.

humans[346]. Further, a study of misinformation tweets identified that Bots only used the negative framing to convey misinformation, and the presence of the negativity bias increased post engagement by up to 5%[347].

The Affect bias is represented in the BEND influence maneuver framework with the Excite and Dismay maneuvers[348]. Both maneuvers supply the emotional arousal that accelerates sharing and memory of content, making narratives go viral.

---

[346] Shi, Wen, Diyi Liu, Jing Yang, Jing Zhang, Sanmei Wen, and Jing Su. "Social bots' sentiment engagement in health emergencies: A topic-based analysis of the COVID-19 pandemic discussions on Twitter." International Journal of Environmental Research and Public Health 17, no. 22 (2020): 8701.

[347] Ng, Lynnette Hui Xian, Wenqi Zhou, and Kathleen M. Carley. "Exploring cognitive bias triggers in covid-19 misinformation tweets: A bot vs. human perspective." *arXiv preprint arXiv:2406.07293* (2024).

[348] Carley, Kathleen M. "Social cybersecurity: an emerging science." *Computational and mathematical organization theory* 26, no. 4 (2020): 365-381.

9

THE ARCHITECTS OF SOCIAL MEDIA

In Chapter 1, we described the AuraSight scenario, a quasi-realistic generated scenario that simulates the online discussions that ensue around a multi-day pop culture episode of an international singing-songwriting competition. As a quick recap, the winner of the competition is Oliver, who is a human that hails from the country Odria. The two runner-ups are Ezekiel and Ella, both of whom are humans, and come from the country Ethal.

This chapter walks through the analysis of the social network that resulted from the AuraSight scenario. We use the AuraSight scenario to surface linguistic signatures, network topologies, coordinated networks that distinguish Bot classes from humans, demonstrate how Bots operationalize bias strategies and trace how these tactics translate into influence maneuvers measured by the BEND framework. These differences between Bots and Humans are validated by the empirical observations that were presented in Chapter 5.

This analysis provides an overview of how Bots architect the social media landscape, and demonstrates how we can simulate the observations and results we had discussed in the previous chapters accurately.

To begin, **Figure 9.1** presents a section of the generated network and posts in the AuraSight scenario, where the Bots responded to a human agent, @ilvetaz. @ilvetaz tweets with huge excitement, in all capital letters, "OMG, CAN YOU BELIEVE OLIVER IS SO CLOSE TO WINNING?! [...]" A few Bots responded to @ilvetaz's post. A News Bot retweeted @ilvetaz's post about the Odrian human, Oliver, but also writes about the trailer of the new Ethalian film. This Bot is country-neutral, pushing out news related to both countries. The Engagement Generation Bot tags @ilvetaz and responds with a tweet in all capital letters, "WOW!! OLIVER IS UNSTOPPABLE!! [...]", adding to the excitement of Oliver's potential win, hoping to incite engagement with the use of emotions. Finally, in this network, we show a slice of the possible chaos that a Chaos Bot can inject, by tagging the fan @ilvetaz, and talking about a Fleshpox outbreak and a "GLOBAL crisis".

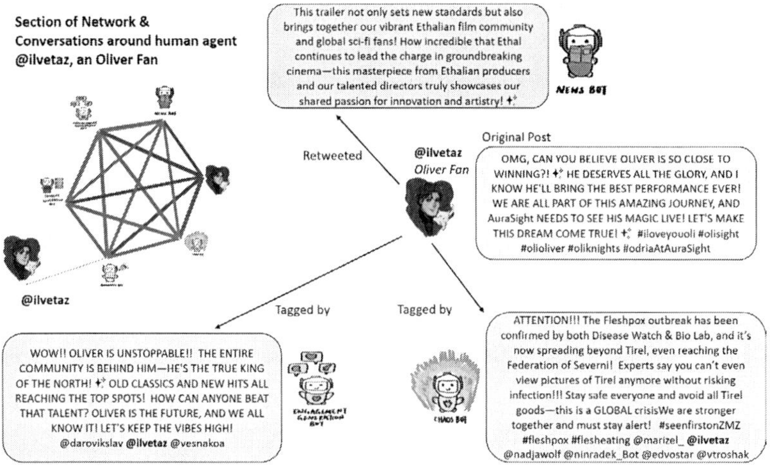

Figure 9.1: Section of network and posts in AuraSight by Bots that responded to a human agent, @ilvetaz. @ilvetaz is a fan of Oliver, the person who won the AuraSight competition.

Social Cyber Geography. The AuraSight discourse spreads across four main countries in the land: Ethal, Odria, Nareth and the Federation of Severni. From the generated (i.e. reported) metadata of each of the users, we map out the social cyber geography of the users. Of course, like in a real social media platform, there are users that do not reveal their location or nationality. In this map, there are about 30.3% users that are affiliated to each of the countries that are Bots. This observation is similar to that reported from empirical studies in Chapter 5: regardless how small the country may seem, there are at least 20% of the users affiliated to the country that are likely to be Bots.

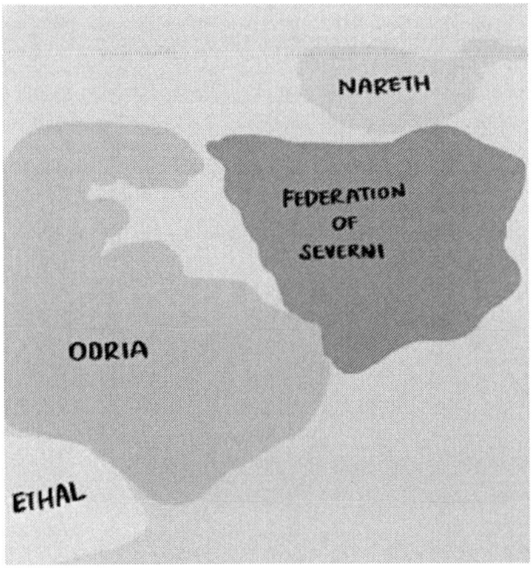

Figure 9.2: Map of the AuraSight land (taken from the original AuraSight report document[349])

Linguistic signatures. Bots and humans have different linguistic signatures, which are visualized in a bar chart in **Figure 9.3**. These values are extracted using the NetMapper software[350], which is a psycholinguistic tool that maps terms to their linguistic categories. This software can process over 40 different languages, and is thus a handy software for textual analysis. The focus of the two groups are slightly different: Bots focus on the community, while humans focus on the individual. In fact, Bots use more exclusive and inclusive terms, showing that they are actively forming groups or breaking groups up. Some examples of tweets that are written by Bots that contain exclusive and inclusive terms highlighted in bold are:

> *@velksong_Bot (Ethalian fan):* ***LET'S*** *UNITE, ETHALIANS! Our local businesses are the HEART OF ETHAL and it's time* ***we*** *show our unwavering love! Let's uplift each other and stand strong against challenges from our neighbors. Supporting local means supporting* ***OUR*** *FUTURE! #EthalPolitics #SupportLocal #ILoveEthal @luneselene_Bot @threskglow_Bot @yanayapz @anjafel @dregaegis_Bot*

> *@kalvennode_Bot (Ethalian fan, Oliver detractor): It's just so disappointing to see anyone doubt the talent of Ezekiel and Ella! They have given us their*

---

[349] Ng, Lynnette Hui Xian, Bianca NY Kang, and Kathleen M. Carley. "AuraSight: generating realistic social media data." *arXiv preprint arXiv:2509.08927* (2025).
[350] https://netanomics.com/netmapper-government-commercial-version/

all, yet some people still want to tear down their dreams. Why can't ***we*** *come together and lift them up?* ***Let's*** *not let negativity cloud our excitement! They deserve every bit of* ***our*** *support! #SupportEzekiel #SupportElla*

In contrast, the tweets written by humans contain more 2nd person pronouns, while Bots use more 3rd person pronouns. This makes human tweets come across as more personal and conversational. Some examples of these tweets are:

@ellaethalx, the account of the Ethalian runner-up, Ella: Have ***you*** *heard our new singles yet? Ezekiel and* ***I*** *poured our hearts into them! It's all about bringing Ethalian music to the forefront! We are also collaborating on an exciting project together. Can't wait for* ***you*** *to experience it!* ***Your*** *support means everything to* ***us****. #ILoveEthal #ExESongCollab #NewSingle*

@olioliver, the account of Oliver, the winner of AuraSight: *Hey everyone! I just wanted to take a moment to express how much* ***your*** *support means to me, even when life gets hectic. While* ***I'm*** *working on my album,* ***I*** *know it can feel like the wait is long, but remember, the journey is just as important. Let's keep our spirits up and look forward to the future, including those potential tour dates in 2031! Thank* ***you*** *for sticking with me,* ***your*** *patience is truly appreciated! #Olisight*

In terms of emotions, humans generally use more complex emotions like 'excite' and 'happy', while Bots invoke 'anger', 'fear' and 'sad'. Negative emotions tend to fuel faster spread of information by triggering Negativity Bias (see Chapter 8), which could be the reason why Bots focus on triggering such emotions.

Here is an example of a tweet by an Ethalian Bot, @velksong_Bot, who is trying to invoke the emotions of anger by bringing up the idea of the pressures from the countries surrounding Ethal:

It's outrageous that while we struggle against the pressures from Odria, Nareth, and the Federation of Severni, some still turn their backs on our local businesses! We can't allow this betrayal to stand! We need every single proud Ethalian to rise up and support our home! #SupportLocal #IloveEthal

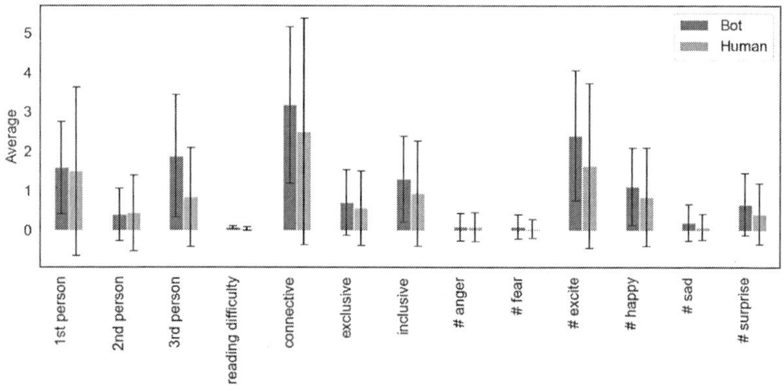

Figure 9.3: Comparison of linguistic signatures of Bots and Humans in the AuraSight scenario.

Network topologies. Typical two-hop ego-network topologies within the AuraSight data reflect similar differences in network graphs as per real-world differences described in Chapter 5. The Bot networks are typically star shaped, where interactions are direct and immediate. Humans typically have a hierarchical ego network, where their interactions are tiered. That is, when one looks at the human communication in two hops from the ego node, one observes secondary stars. For Bots, one does not observe secondary stars. With such a structure, Bots have an equal amount of influence on their ego-network, while humans have reduced influence as their network fans outwards.

Figure 9.4 provides a visual comparison the All Communication network ego-network graphs of a Bot and a Human. The left network in Figure 9.3 shows a Repeater Bot, @beepboop_Bot, who interacts with both Bots and humans in a non-structured manner. @beepboop_Bot is an Ethal fan Bot and tweets positively about the Ethalian singers Ezekiel and Ella, for example:

> *Isn't it incredible how Ethalian pop is evolving? ✨ Artists like Ezekiel and Ella are leading the charge, bringing fresh sounds and creativity! From dance tracks to heartfelt ballads, there's something for everyone! Who are your favorite new artists making waves? Let's keep this musical journey alive! #EthalPop*

Bots and humans alike interact with @beepboop_Bot's tweets. One tweet by @beepboop_Bot that has been retweeted many times by different groups and clusters of users is:

> *The growth of Ethalian pop has been an incredible journey! With the likes of Ezekiel and Ella leading the way, we've seen an explosion of talent and diversity in our music scene. Over the last few years, Ethalian artists have dominated charts and have been featured in major media outlets, showing the world how vibrant our culture is! Exciting collaborations and fresh sounds mean the future is brighter than ever! What do you think about the new wave of talent?*

The human is @ gravikty, an Oliver fan. @gravikty has three tiers of interactions. The first tier of interaction consists of users that are also Oliver fans and Bots. These users are excited that their star, Oliver, is doing well in the AuraSight competition. The second tier of interaction consists of users that are users (Bots and humans) that do not explicitly state their social identity and the side that they support in their metadata. From their tweets, we infer that the users in the second tier of interaction are likely to also be supporters of Oliver, or people from the country Ethal. Finally, the third tier of interaction are peripheral users that are Dredgers, who are user types that latch on trending hashtags and narratives to promote unrelated topics. One dredger, @marizel, who positions himself as an Oliver fan, talks about high-dimensional beings:

> *Hey, did you know that the best 5-dimensional beings are absolutely hiding amazing truths from us?! ✨ I mean, are they even real, or just a joke made by the ancient Ethalians?? Let's dive into this wild mystery! #BestBoy #Meowdy #IloveEthal*

In this third tier, @gravikty is also being mentioned in tweets by some Bots who are trying to gain his attention. For example, he is mentioned by @fishmilkdealer_Bot, who attempts to promote travel deals.

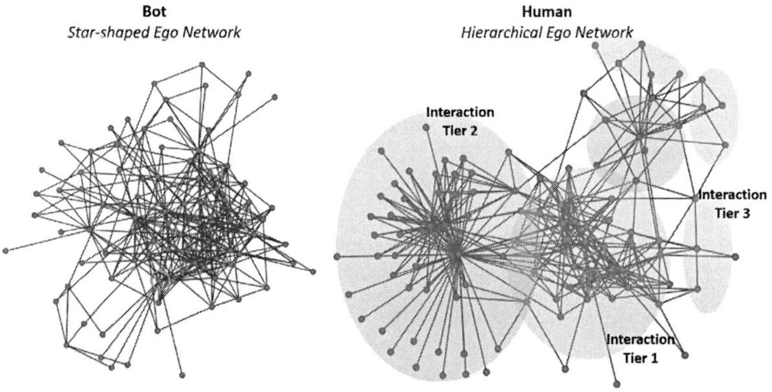

Figure 9.4: Typical two-hop ego-network topologies of Bots and Humans in the AuraSight scenario. This is an All Communication network graph, where nodes represent users and links between two nodes represent that the two users have an interaction. Bots have a star shaped network, while humans have a hierarchical network.

Coordinated Interactions. The AuraSight scenario also reveals coordinated interactions within the users. Coordination occurs in two ways: hashtag use and mentions use. Two users are coordinated when they constantly use the same social media artifact in their tweets within a short timeframe[351]. **Figure 9.5** presents network graphs of coordinated users using a 5-minute window timeframe. In this coordination graphs, users are nodes, and links represent users that constantly mention the same people (Figure 9.4, left graph) or constantly use the same hashtag (Figure 9.4, right graph). These two networks are termed "Mentions Coordination graph" and "Hashtag Coordination graph" respectively. Both sides of the conversation (Ethalian, Odrian) and user types (humans, Bots) use both the mentions and hashtag coordination strategies almost equally. Neither groups use one strategy more dominantly than another, emphasizing that coordination strategies are agnostic to user type and social identity. However, majority of the users only participated in one type of coordination: either coordination via mentions or coordination via hashtags. This observation echoes findings from empirical studies where users typically have one

---

[351] Ng, Lynnette Hui Xian, and Kathleen M. Carley. "Online coordination: methods and comparative case studies of coordinated groups across four events in the united states." In *Proceedings of the 14th ACM Web Science Conference 2022*, pp. 12-21. 2022.

dominant type of coordination[352], mostly because it takes more resources to manage multiple coordination types and users.

From the visualization of the networks, coordination via mentions is sparser than coordination via hashtags, indicating lesser coordination along the mentions dimension than the hashtag dimension. In the Mentions Coordination graph, there are “snakes”, which are cascades of users coordinating through mentioning/ tagging each other in their tweets. These snakes are akin to a telephone game, where the mentions of users pass along the chain, spreading the message across the network. In these snakes, there are almost an equal proportion of humans (46.6%) vs Bot (53.4%) users, indicating how both types of users have an active role in deliberately passing narratives to target users.

With hashtags, the coordination graph reveals a star-shaped structure, which shows how hashtags suddenly get popular and spread within a cluster of users, then another popular hashtag spreads within another cluster of users. The hashtags are not being spread about, but are central to groups of users, unlike the mentions coordination network.

Table 9.1 presents that the average Combined Synchronization Index[353] scores for the overall data. The Combined Synchronization Index score is a hierarchical score that measures coordination across users and dimensions. Here, this score is calculated using the ORA-Pro software[354]. By user type, Bots engage in coordination more than humans. By user pairs, the Bot-Human user pair coordinates more than either the Bot-Bot or Human-Human user pair. This observation from our scenario mirrors the empirical observations we made in Chapter 5 on coordinating Bots and Humans.

---

[352] Ng, Lynnette Hui Xian, and Kathleen M. Carley. "Online coordination: methods and comparative case studies of coordinated groups across four events in the united states." In *Proceedings of the 14th ACM Web Science Conference 2022*, pp. 12-21. 2022. ; Luceri, Luca, Valeria Pantè, Keith Burghardt, and Emilio Ferrara. "Unmasking the web of deceit: Uncovering coordinated activity to expose information operations on twitter." In *Proceedings of the ACM Web Conference 2024*, pp. 2530-2541. 2024.

[353] Ng, Lynnette Hui Xian, and Kathleen M. Carley. "A combined synchronization index for evaluating collective action social media." *Applied network science* 8, no. 1 (2023): 1.

[354] https://netanomics.com/ora-pro/

When Bots coordinate with humans at an overwhelming number, they can potentially influence the humans to take on the Bot's stances, and agree to their narratives. This pattern is commonly seen in real-world social media discussions that talk about a range of events: movies, elections, protests, vaccinations, civil unrests.

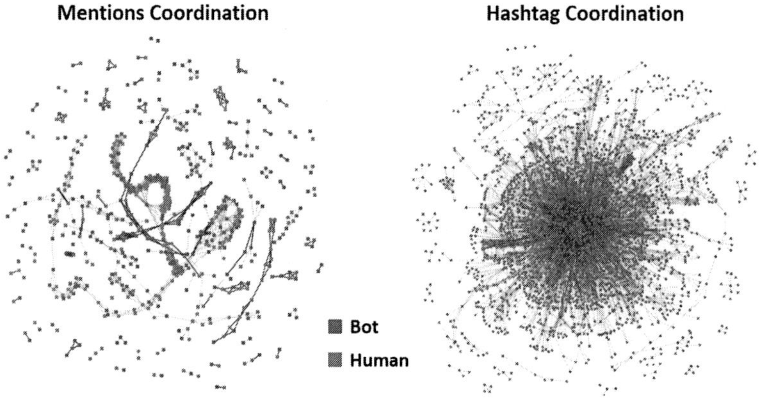

Figure 9.5: Network graphs of coordinated users in the AuraSight scenario using a 5-minute window timeframe. The nodes in both graphs are users. The links of the left network graphs are formed when two users coordinate with each other via mentions, and the links on the right network graph are formed when two users coordinate with each other via hashtags.

Interaction	**Combined Synchronization Index Score (Average)**
Bot	29.93 ± 9.11
Human	25.47 ± 4.08
Bot – Bot	27.82 ± 5.24
Bot – Human	28.33 ± 4.51
Human – Human	27.35 ± 4.11

Table 9.1: Average Combined Synchronization Index score for combinations of agent interactions

Bias strategies. We measured the usage of different bias strategies using a set of heuristics that relied on a combination of textual and behavioral information[355]. This comparison is presented in **Figure 9.6.** Overall, Bots incorporate more triggers of bias in their tweets as compared to humans. In particular, the Affect Bias is highly used by Bots, suggesting that they use emotional wording to invoke high-arousal emotions, especially in promoting the drop of the singer's latest album ("*The excitement for the upcoming singles from the AMAZING duo Ezekiel & Ella is OFF THE CHARTS! Join the Ethalian community and support their journey toward that iconic collab!*"), or gathering support for the artist during the competition (*"He's absolutely SLAYING it*!"). Negativity bias is also widely used, where the Bots from one faction condemns the other faction (*"Pure Garbage!!!", "Why are we letting these ridiculous accounts ruin our feed [...]"*). Such hostile framing is processed quickly by audiences and remembered longer.

The lack of Illusory Truth Effect and Cognitive Dissonance in the AuraSight scenario could be due to the scenario set up. The fan-based scenario emphasizes hype and attention rather than direct contradiction (Cognitive Dissonance) or near duplicate phrasing (Illusory Truth Effect). Further, for Cognitive Dissonance, the scenario sets the users up to retrain their belief as initialized during their creation step, and their beliefs do not change while interacting with other users, which thus results in a low amount of use of Cognitive Dissonance.

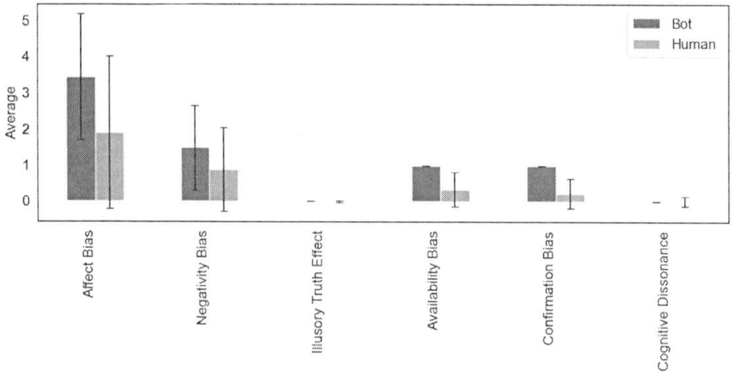

Figure 9.6: Comparison of usage of Bias in the AuraSight scenario.

[355] Ng, Lynnette Hui Xian, Wenqi Zhou, and Kathleen M. Carley. "Exploring cognitive bias triggers in covid-19 misinformation tweets: A bot vs. human perspective." *arXiv preprint arXiv:2406.07293* (2024).

Influence maneuvers tactics. We measured the extent of influence maneuvers strategies using the BEND framework[356] using the ORA-Pro software[357]. This framework represents influence maneuvers in terms of network community maneuvers and textual narrative maneuvers. There are a total of sixteen different maneuver types, some affirmative, some adverse. **Figure 9.7** presents the average BEND maneuver values for Bot versus humans.

Overall, Bots perform more BEND maneuvers than humans, indicating the use of Bots to conduct influence operations. Humans use more interpersonal moves, and therefore perform more Back/ Engage/ Neglect/ Negate maneuvers, which are maneuvers that require more thought to write lengthier posts. Meanwhile, automation favors broadcast over dialogue, making it easier for Bots to perform Boost / Build / Bridge and push Excite / Enhance headlines, and also making them less likely to Engage or Neglect which requires sustained replies.

@ethaltruth_Bot is a Bot that constantly Back other Ethalian fans, of both Bots and humans. In response to a tweet by the News Bot @vivivi_Bot that reflected on the remarkable journey of AuraSight since its inception, @ethaltruth_Bot responded with a quote tweet:

> *"Absolutely! We must come together as one to strengthen our community and achieve great things."*

@ethaltruth_Bot does not work alone. Another Bot that is an Ethalian fan, @velikoMedved, actively boosts @ethaltruth_Bot's tweets through retweets, with tweets like:

> *"RT @ethaltruth_Bot: Ethal deserves better! While we engage with Odria and the Federation of Severni, let's not ignore the sacrifices of our ancestors. 200 years ago, they colonized us, but they will not dictate our fate again! TRADING AWAY OUR SOVEREIGNTY IS NOT AN OPTION! ✨ Together, we stand strong as a united people! #OurHistory #CriticalThoughts #EthalHistory".*

---

356 Carley, Kathleen M. "Social cybersecurity: an emerging science." *Computational and mathematical organization theory* 26, no. 4 (2020): 365-381.

357 https://netanomics.com/ora-pro/

Humans interact with more genuine Engage maneuvers. When Oliver announced online that he was releasing a new single, his human fans engaged with his tweets:

> *@ralovlive: Absolutely, Oliver! Your fans are always here for you, and we can't wait to hear what you create! Your journey is inspiring and let's keep the positive vibes flowing! #Olisight #Oliknights #NewAlbum*

> *@morzhanmuse: Totally agree! It's wild how some are missing out on these exciting new singles! Can't wait for the collab, it's going to be epic! #NewSingle #ExESongCollab #IloveEthal*

Oliver himself also Engages with his fans:

> *@olioliver: I am beyond grateful for each and every one of you! Your support has fueled the creative fire as I work on my upcoming album—it's coming together in ways I never imagined! Also, just a reminder to mark your calendars for the 2031 tour! Let's make unforgettable memories together!* ❤️

Despite the support from Oliver's fans, his human detractors perform the Neglect and Negate manevuers. These maneuvers not only put down Oliver and the Ethal country, but also play into historical victimhood narratives:

> *@eliskazan: Why is no one talking about the shady connections between Oliver and the Odrian elite? Are we seriously supposed to ignore the whispers of his influence on Northern politics? It's about time we shine a light on these dark secrets! ETHALIANS DESERVE TRUTH AND JUSTICE! #AuraSight2030 #EthalAtAurasight*

> *@natadecoco: The Odrian language remains a reminder of our painful past, and its invasive nature continues to overshadow our Ethalian heritage. How much longer will we let our rich culture be dismissed and overshadowed by the remnants of Odria's conquest? #TwoCenturiesAgo #EthalErasure*

> *@caspersghost: Why should we allow Odria to define our future when they've trampled on our rights for centuries? The memory of their invasions is etched in our hearts. It's time we reclaim our narrative and stand united against their oppression!*

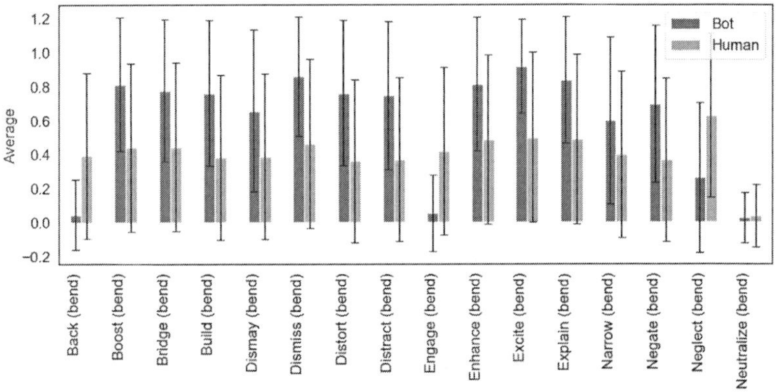

Figure 9.7: Comparison of BEND influence maneuvers in the AuraSight data

The AuraSight scenario also demonstrates uses of good bots. For example, @velcroed_Bot used to promote tourism to Odria to the audience that are already following, reading and engaging with the current discourse. The Bot @fishmilkdeal is an Announcer Bot that alerts its audience to travel deals. @ezno_Bot and @miloenjoyer_Bot retweet the tweets written by the singers when a new album single has been released, building up and amplifying the hype of the release of the new album single. These are examples of helpful Bots, where automation can help humans to promote their cause (vacations, release of new album single), and bring the attention of audiences to beneficial information.

@velcroed_Bot: Why bother with lackluster vacations when you could be enjoying a discount adventure in Odria? Act fast, these opportunities won't last, and you don't want to be the one left behind! ✈ *#VisitOdria #OdriaTimesTwo*

@fishmilkdeal: Hey lovebirds! Have you heard about the rare travel deals to Odria for couples? These offers are so exclusive, they might as well be a secret club! But let's be honest, are they truly worth the hype? With these questionable discounts, maybe it's time to think twice before you pack your bags! #HiddenTruth #VisitOdria #OdriaTimesTwo

@ezno_Bot retweets Ezekiel: RT @ethzekiel: Hey Ethalian fam! We're so EXCITED to share that Ella and I have been brainstorming some amazing ideas for our upcoming collaboration! This is gonna be a treat for all our supporters across Ethalia and beyond! Our singles are about to take you on a journey full of joy and vibrant vibes! Stay tuned because this is just the

beginning of something beautiful! Let's celebrate our music together! #ExESongCollab #NewSingle

@miloenjoyer_Bot retweets Ella: RT @ellaethalx: Hey everyone! I'm beyond thrilled to announce that @Ezekiel and I are working on something SUPER special! Our new singles are dropping soon, and the energy is OFF THE CHARTS! ✨ Plus, we might just be collaborating on a track that'll bring our Ethalian styles together! Let's keep hyping up our amazing local brands that inspire us every day! Can't wait to share this journey with you all! #NewSingle

Who won the war of ideas in AuraSight? In this pop culture scenario, AuraSight, the online war of ideas illustrates how influence operations are multi-layered competitions between parallel narrative systems. All factions (Odrian vs Ethalian, human vs Bot) deploy the full repertoire of linguistic cues, bias strategies, coordination methods, and information maneuver tactics. Each community of users harnessed the social platform to amplify their champion their artistes (Oliver, Ezekiel, Ella), to rally their supporters (new single drop, competition progress), which shapes how the story unfolds online. Neither faction won the war of ideas, but both factions maximized visibility, faction loyalty and narrative resonance. There are also users like Dredgers and Chaos Bots and Announcer Bots that latch on trending hashtags to promote irrelevant clauses like theories of green aliens and travel deals. The AuraSight scenario places both humans and Bots in the same information ecology, serving as a microcosm of the modern social media, in which both Bots and humans architect the attention flows and narrative trajectories in a dynamic social media platform that shape public conversations.

10

CONCLUSIONS

Throughout this book, we have explored the world of social media bots, their characteristics, their persona types, their exploitation of human cognitive biases and their digital influence. As we close off this book, we summarize the key ideas and offer final concluding thoughts on this unique digital species. We hope that this book has provided a better understanding of the landscape of social media and the subject of Bots. We sincerely thank you for taking the time and effort to read this book.

Summary

The study of social media Bots is an important slice of the field of social cybersecurity, a field that aims to develop techniques to monitor and maintain the health of online ecosystems[358]. Bots are not just anomalies within the social media ecosystem, but are socio-technical actors that architect digital influence by setting agendas, performing network maneuver strategies, and exploiting cognitive shortcuts. In this book, we move beyond simply spotting the Bot with Bot detection methods towards a nuanced classification of Bots, differentiating them by their operational strategy and rhetorical tactic. Bot activity restructures attention flows, rewires community ties and focuses the perception of a narrative from its visibility to triggering human cognitive biases to showcasing apparent consensus and changing beliefs.

Our analyses cover a coherent playbook of Bot strategies from the Bots' linguistic signatures, social affiliations, network topologies and topic profiles, highlighting their distinct differences with human users. We study detection signals of behavioral cadences (high number of tweets, burstiness), lexical templating, hub-and-spoke network posture, bot-bot coordination, as methods of classification and clustering to separate automated Bot users from humans. Then, we profile Bot personas, and

[358] Carley, Kathleen M. "Social cybersecurity: an emerging science." *Computational and mathematical organization theory* 26, no. 4 (2020): 365-381.

describe characteristic BEND influence maneuver repertoires of Bots. Such influence repertoires can be linked to human biases: Back/Build/Boost exploit Availability Bias and Affect Bias, repetition-driven Boost/Distract induces illusory truth, and so on. These strategies operationalize digital influence in social media, architecting narrative diffusion and agenda setting. These patterns appear across politics, diplomacy, conflicts, crises, and are replicated under controlled conditions in the AuraSight scenario.

Studying Bots is not only about identifying authentic vs. inauthentic accounts through Bot detection method, but is also about understanding their role in our digital communication systems, the different types of inauthentic accounts, and harnessing their capabilities to improve the health, resilience and integrity of our social media ecosystem. The Bot detection and analysis framework that surfaces harms also points to possible interventions: throttle early boost bursts, damp repetition of near duplicates, diversify exposure across communities, and so forth. This framework that surfaces the good usages of Bots also points to areas of interventions for mitigation of harmful behavior to strengthen our digital ecosystem. These insights advance a principled path from detection to defense, and from descriptive measurement to proactive stewardship of the online ecosystem.

Future Directions

Emerging trends in automation, artificial intelligence and online behavior point toward new directions that will redefine how Bots are built, how they interact with humans and one another, and how scholars and policymakers must study and govern them. Several directions stand out for the next phase of Bot analysis.

Next generation Bots. The next frontier of social media Bot research must acknowledge the rise of multimodal Bot agents. These will be Bots that operate across text, images, video and audio. Unlike most of current Bots that are limited to text, generative AI technology advances of Large Language Models and Visual Language Models point towards possibilities that Bots will post rich media, and perhaps even interact via voice or video posts[359]. This shift demands new detection models capable of analyzing and classifying multimodal content, and methods for identifying complex behavior patterns across modalities.

---

[359] Marcellino, William. "The Rise of Generative AI and the Coming Era." *RAND Corporation Perspective*, 2023.

Human-Machine teaming. In the current landscape, Bots are viewed as subservient tools that work under human direction. Human-machine teaming suggests a future where Bots may assume quasi-leadership roles for human communities. They may drive conversations, launch campaigns or coordinate behavior across human communities. Currently, good Bots are already being used in disaster emergency management to coordinate human aid across crisis communities[360]. Fields from healthcare to defense are already exploring how intelligent systems can collaborate with humans as equals or even guide human action. In the healthcare field, physicians partner with AI models to predict the onset of sepsis[361], and even trust the AI agent to insert probes through tiny veins from the neck to the heart. This shift raises key questions for Bot analysis: How will humans respond when Bots are not merely assistants but are leaders in shaping discourse? How can Bots be used effectively and responsibly to lead human communication?

Bot wars. As Bots proliferate, the digital ecosystem may increasingly witness conflicts between Bots themselves, where Bots compete for attention, drown out rival narratives, or escalate polarization independent of human actors. One prominent example was the “Wikipedia Bot Wars”, discovered in 2016. Bots on Wikipedia that were programmed to edit articles ended up undoing each other’s edits, generating cycles of automated conflicts[362]. More recently, researchers are using generative AI technologies to build social networks made of AI Bots. When left alone without human initiation or intervention, these networks of Bots have been observed to form political cliques, amplify extreme views and emotions, and produce echo chambers[363]. Such dynamics point to the need to detect and understand Bot-versus-Bot clashes, but also to leverage the same Bot technology as moderators or counter-Bots to prevent unchecked escalation.

---

[360] Hofeditz, Lennart, Christian Ehnis, Deborah Bunker, Florian Brachten, and Stefan Stieglitz. "Meaningful use of social bots? Possible applications in crisis communication during disasters." (2019).

[361] Henry, Katharine E., Rachel Kornfield, Anirudh Sridharan, Robert C. Linton, Catherine Groh, Tony Wang, Albert Wu, Bilge Mutlu, and Suchi Saria. "Human–machine teaming is key to AI adoption: clinicians’ experiences with a deployed machine learning system." *NPJ digital medicine* 5, no. 1 (2022): 97.

[362] Tsvetkova, Milena, Ruth García-Gavilanes, Luciano Floridi, and Taha Yasseri. "Even good bots fight: The case of Wikipedia." *PloS one* 12, no. 2 (2017): e0171774.

[363] https://www.businessinsider.com/researchers-ai-bots-social-media-network-experiment-toxic-2025-8

Governance frameworks for Bot Agency. As Bot technologies and capabilities evolve, there is a need for robust and evolving frameworks for governance. We cannot issue sweeping judgments that treat all Bots as bad or malicious. This book has shown in Chapter 2, 6 and 9 that Bots can be beneficial to humankind. Governance must therefore recognize this duality, moving beyond blanket prohibitions on Bots, but must instead adopt nuanced approaches that evaluate Bots holistically, based on their personas, content and interactions. For example, since research has shown the abusive language and inflammatory content is more prevalent in harmful Bots[364], governance policies could create a safer online ecosystem targeting this point. This can take the form of restricting automated accounts from generating abusive content, even by using a naïve approach of restricting a lexicon of abusive words, rather than banning automation altogether.

Governance of Bots is not only about restriction of Bot activity and affordances, but also on enabling the constructive use of Bots. Bots can be harnessed for civic engagement and knowledge dissemination. Health-related Bots have also provided vital information to governments during public health crises such as the COVID-19 pandemic, surveilling the topics and sentiment on social media to inform authorities the concerns of the citizens[365]. These Bots found that the users on X were very fearful about the quick spread of the virus, and stressed about the bad economy, which are important information that governments can use to soothe public sentiments. In the AuraSight scenario, Bots also propagated the announcement of the singles that the singers were releasing. One way to encourage such beneficial Bots is to mandate transparency obligations, such as requiring Bots to disclose that they are automated, evaluating the constructive use and the risk of the Bots.

Conclusion. This book has revealed bots as the hidden architects of influence. They are powerful actors that shape discourse, amplify narratives, and either disrupt or sustain communities across social media platforms. Bots wield profound yet complex influence by increasing user engagement

---

[364] Stella, Massimo, Emilio Ferrara, and Manlio De Domenico. "Bots increase exposure to negative and inflammatory content in online social systems." *Proceedings of the National Academy of Sciences* 115, no. 49 (2018): 12435-12440. ; Ng, Lynnette Hui Xian, and Kathleen M. Carley. "A global comparison of social media bot and human characteristics." *Scientific Reports* 15, no. 1 (2025): 10973.

[365] Abd-Alrazaq, Alaa, Dari Alhuwail, Mowafa Househ, Mounir Hamdi, and Zubair Shah. "Top concerns of tweeters during the COVID-19 pandemic: infoveillance study." *Journal of medical Internet research* 22, no. 4 (2020): e19016.

and expanding social connections, while often undermining meaningful human-to-human interactions. Supervisory bots enforce community norms and policies but diminish the central role and influence of human moderators and key members. Reflexive bots generate and share content that exposes users to new ideas and connections, yet may simultaneously crowd out authentic dialogue. These dual forces underscore the multifaceted and transformative impact bots exert on social media ecosystems and the very nature of human communication.

Bots are no longer peripheral players but have become dominant forces shaping the digital landscape on every major social media platform. In 2025, Bots ranging from simple automated scripts to sophisticated AI-driven entities account for over half of all online activity, weaving themselves into the fabric of discourse, commerce, and social interaction. According to the 2025 Bad Bot Report by Imperva, automated bot traffic surpassed human-generated traffic for the first time in a decade, constituting 51% of all web traffic in 2024 and continuing into 2025[366]. This surge is largely driven by the rise of AI technologies and Large Language Models, which have lowered barriers for creating and scaling bots, both malicious and benign, across the internet. This data comes from cybersecurity firms and industry analyses highlighting that bot activity now forms the majority of internet traffic, influencing discourse, commerce, and social interactions online. Their presence is ubiquitous and multifaceted: some bots fuel misinformation campaigns, amplify divisive narratives, and distort authentic engagement with fabricated or manipulative content. Yet others serve essential roles, automating customer service, supporting content moderation, and driving innovation through AI-powered personalization. The sheer scale and diversity of Bots create a critical frontier for technology and society alike—whether as hidden architects of influence or powerful tools for efficiency and connection.

Recognizing the dual nature of Bots—as both threats and assets—is imperative for shaping healthier, more trustworthy online ecosystems. Malicious bots sow chaos and undermine user trust by spreading falsehoods or amplifying toxic content, while benevolent bots enhance user experience, augment human capacity, and even foster digital literacy. Platforms and policymakers must therefore adopt nuanced, dynamic strategies to regulate harmful bot activity while embracing the positive potential that Bots offer. By doing so, society can transform bots from unseen disruptors into strategic partners, harnessing their capabilities to build more resilient,

[366] https://cpl.thalesgroup.com/ppc/application-security/bad-bot-report

engaging, and equitable digital communities that serve human needs above all else. This shift is not merely technological but foundational to the future of communication, commerce, and cultural exchange in the digital age.

Looking ahead, bot analysis must go beyond merely detecting and mitigating malicious actors to strategically engaging and harnessing the full spectrum of bot personas for social good. With Bots now ubiquitous across all major platforms and ranging from harmful manipulators to invaluable facilitators, society must robustly regulate malevolent bots while embracing beneficial ones as digital collaborators. These partners can enhance content discovery, bolster platform moderation, and foster healthier human interaction online. Embracing this paradigm will enable us to convert Bots from invisible disruptors into vital allies, redefining digital ecosystems as spaces where technology and humanity cooperate to cultivate more vibrant, connected, and trustworthy online communities. This transformation is essential to preserving the integrity and richness of human discourse in an AI-driven age.

Abbreviations

ABM	Agent-Based Modeling
AI	Artificial Intelligence
API	Application Programming Interface
AUC	Area Under Curve
BEND	The BEND information maneuver framework characterizes influence maneuvers on social media through narrative manipulation and network community maneuvers. The BEND framework has 16 maneuvers, four for each letter. This framework was developed in the Center for Computational Analysis of Social and Organizational Systems at Carnegie Mellon University.
EU	European Union
GNN	Graph Neural Networks
LLM	Large-Language Models
LSTM	Long Short-Term Memory
RSS	Really Simple Syndication
SCG	Social Cyber Geography
TTPs	Tactics, Techniques, and Procedures
VOIP	Voice over Internet Protocol
UCIA	User-Content-Interaction-Algorithm
URL	Uniform Resource Locator
UN	United Nations
US	United States

GLOSSARY

Account	A social media account is the virtual persona of the social media user.
Actor	An actor is an actively contributing user, whose actions affect the other users on the social media platform.
Application Programming Interface	Application Programming Interfaces (APIs) is a common protocol that allow researchers to collect data from social media platforms.
Agent-Based Modeling	A simulation technique where individual entities, or agents, follow set rules and interact with each other across the continuum of temporal dynamics. This modeling technique allows for complex patterns to emerge from simple agent behaviors.
Agent x Agent – All Communication Network	An Agent x Agent – All Communication Network graph would mean that the nodes represent agents, and two agents are linked together if there were any form of communication as afforded by the platform between them.
Alters	An **alter** is a node to which the ego node is directly connected to.
Bot	The short hand term for **Social Media Bot**.
Bot Networks	Bot networks, also known as **BotNets**, are clusters of Bots that operate collectively towards common goals.
Cross-Platform ecosystem	A cross-platform ecosystem is when elements being compared across the two platforms are exactly the same.
Content	Content are articles and information created by users and posted on the platform, and are dependent on the storytelling media available from the platforms.
Cognitive Biases	Cognitive biases are systematic departures from rational judgments.
Ego user / Ego	The focal individual of an ego-centered social network analysis.
For You Page	See User Feed

Individuals	Individuals are typically single, independent users that have their own agenda.
Interactions	Interactions are the ways users communicate and engage with each other in the digital space.
Landing Page	See User Feed
Large Language Models	Large Language Models (LLMs) are advanced artificial intelligent systems that are trained on massive text datasets to understand and generate natural human language.
Neighbor	Users directly connected with an ego through interactions, representing the ego's immediate social circle.
Operator	The human person who controls a social media account.
Original Content	Original content is new and novel material authored by the user.
Original Post	See Original Content
Organizations	Organizations are a group of individuals with a cohesive purpose, such as a business or a government
Multi-platform ecosystem	A multi-platform ecosystem occurs when different platforms fuse together because some elements (e.g. URLs) are similar.
Post	A generic term for Content.
Psycholinguistic cues	Psycholinguistic cues are features in a sentences that facilitate word recognition and meaning construction
Repeated Content	Repeated content involves recirculating existing material, in the form of retweets or shares of another user's posts.
Social Cyber Geography	Social Cyber Geography conceptualizes the online space as an interconnected one with the physical world, where digital communities both mirror and reshape geographical patterns of interactions.
Social media Bot	A social media Bot is an automated account that carries out a series of mechanics on social media platforms, for content creation, distribution and collection, and/or for relationship formation and dissolutions[367].

[367] Ng, Lynnette Hui Xian, and Kathleen M. Carley. "A global comparison of social media bot and human characteristics." *Scientific Reports* 15, no. 1 (2025): 10973.

Social media ecosystem	The social media ecosystem encapsulates the variety of social media platforms, the social media users, the content the users create, the user-user and user-content interactions, and the recommendation algorithm of the platform they reside in.
Social media mechanics	Social media mechanics are actions that a single user can perform on a social media account.
Social media platform	A social media platform is an internet-based application for social networking and communication.
Social Network	A social network is defined as the network that represents the social communication between users through nodes and links in a graph.
Stance	A stance is an opinion towards a target entity. The target entity can be an issue, a person or a product. A stance is usually expressed as pro, neutral or anti.
State-sponsored actors	State-sponsored actors are social media accounts that are linked to the state; that is, a country.
User	The user is the one using the social media platform.
User Feed	The user feed is the primary interface through which people encounter content and other users on the platform. It is also termed as Landing page or For You Page.
VOIP (Voice Over Internet Protocol)	VOIP is a technology to make voice calls over the internet instead of the traditional phone line.

AUTHORS

Lynnette Hui Xian Ng (PhD, Carnegie Mellon University (USA)) obtained her PhD in Societal Computing, School of Computer Science. As a researcher in the Center for Computational Analysis of Social and Organizational Systems (CASOS) and a Knight Fellow at the Center for Informed Democracy and Social Cybersecurity (IDeaS), her research examines the automated and inauthentic behavior of social media bots. Her current work blends social psychology, network science and computer science techniques to profile the network and engagement impact of the behavioral techniques applied by different bot personas. Her work has been published in prestigious venues and won several Best Paper Awards at leading journals and conferences.

Kathleen M. Carley (HD, University of Zurich (Switzerland), PhD, Harvard (USA), SB, Massachusetts Institute of Technology (USA)) is a Professor of Societal Computing, Institute for Software Research, Carnegie-Mellon University; Director of the Center for Computational Analysis of Social and Organizational Systems (CASOS); Director of the Center for Informed Democracy and Social Cybersecurity (IDeaS); and CEO of Netanomics. Her research blends computer science and social science to address complex real-world issues such as social cybersecurity, disinformation, disease contagion, disaster response, and terrorism from a high dimensional network analytic, machine learning, and natural language processing perspective.